Baptist Campus Ministry at Crossroads

Baptist Campus Ministry at Crossroads

*A Historical and Philosophical Perspective
on Its Diamond Anniversary*

Samuel Sanford Jr.

Foreword by C. William Junker

PROVIDENCE HOUSE PUBLISHERS
Franklin, Tennessee

Selected Scripture taken from the Holy Bible, authorized King James Version; and New Revised Standard Version Bible. Copyright © 1989 Division of Christian Education of the National Council of the Churches of Christ in the United States of America. Used by permission.

Printed in the United States of America

01   00   99   98   97   5   4   3   2   1

ISBN: 1–57736-053-2

Cover design by Bozeman Design

PROVIDENCE HOUSE PUBLISHERS
238 Seaboard Lane • Franklin, Tennessee 37067
800-321-5692

To

G. Avery Lee, Litt. D.
(My LSU BSU Secretary)
now
Pastor Emeritus
St. Charles Avenue Baptist Church
New Orleans, Louisiana

and to

That second generation of Baptist campus ministers
who spent a lifetime on local campuses and retired;

They are among those the writer of Hebrews penned
"of whom the world is not worthy."

CONTENTS

FOREWORD

The time is right for this history to be written. Since the early 1970s when A. Ronald Tonks wrote a brief, fiftieth-year update of Baptist Student Union (BSU) history, no formal account of Southern Baptist student work has been published.

The *time* is right, not only because 1997 is the seventy-fifth anniversary of the founding of the national movement, but also because, as the author has written, Baptist student work (or campus ministry) is at a critical moment in its history. Changing denominational priorities are bringing new pressures. Some current trends and events appear to be signs of declining interest and support.

The national staff of the Sunday School Board's National Student Ministry (NSM), for instance, has been gradually reduced to roughly one-half of its size in 1980, the year I left the department. It has been organized into a less visible entity within the board's organization. The final issue of the venerable *Student* magazine was published in May 1997. As I write this foreword, twenty-five Southern Baptist leaders, chaired by a full-time evangelist—not by the head of NSM—have begun meeting with Campus Crusade for Christ senior staff members to explore new working relationships.

Several state conventions are also in the process of reorganizing. New in-state alignments are not always detrimental to student ministries. In some states the work may benefit from its repositioning. In others, however, student ministries seem to have lost status and/or valuable relationships.

Among Southern Baptist constituency at large, the perennial job of justifying student work's existence continues, but perhaps not in as learning-friendly an environment as in earlier eras. The current atmosphere of constant change keeps the anxiety level and uncertainty index level high.

The time is right for *this* history to be written. More than a logging of chronological facts, Dr. Sanford's "philosophical history" gives an overview of major developments and shifts in the philosophies and basic approaches of Southern Baptist campus ministry as it has found expression during these formative years.

The reader comes away with a deep appreciation for the struggles the movement has had in gaining and maintaining credibility in a denomination that has often favored a single-thrust approach (e.g., evangelism, church-starting, or church growth) rather than the full-orbed Christian growth and outreach program BSU has become—and for the leaders who have persevered in the face of changing societal values, campus cultures, and denominational priorities.

9

Sanford taps into valuable and sometimes obscure sources from the various eras of the movement. References reveal the author's wide readership, not only of relevant Southern Baptist material, but also of a broad range of philosophical and theological analyses of the university and Christian ministry to it.

The time is right for *this author* to have written this history. Sam Sanford's experience bridges the tenures of the major national Baptist student work "secretaries" or "directors" up to the present NSM director, Bill Henry. Sanford was an active "BSUer" at Louisiana State University during the Frank Leavell years. He began his thirty-nine years as a campus minister while the Leavell philosophy was still paramount. His ministry spanned the tenures of Kearnie Keegan, David Alexander, Charles Roselle, and Charles Johnson.

The varying types of campuses he served forced Sanford to grapple personally with the student diversity he discusses in his book and to probe the basic philosophy of BSU. In his writing and speaking to campus ministers through the years—probably as much as any local campus minister of his time—Sanford has been an analyst and critic of the work. He has been a *student* of *student ministries*. His ability to distance himself from the ministry in which he spent his working life is evident in this volume.

Finally, Sam Sanford is an example of what he declares a campus minister should be—a "called" person. For Sanford, campus ministry is not just a job; it has been and is his vocation, a life commitment. He wants the movement to prosper. Consequently, his passion for the work and his discouragement with less than the best circumstances for its vitality are sometimes apparent. These things *matter* to him.

C. William Junker
Former Baptist Campus Minister and
Member, National Student Ministry Staff, 1954–1980

ACKNOWLEDGMENTS

I said in Atlanta during the 1986 banquet of the Association of Southern Baptist Campus Ministers when they honored me as the Campus Minister of the Year, "If I could choose campus ministry again, I would!" However, there were many along the way who have contributed to my work and—not the least—are those who struggled with me to complete this book.

One person who behind the scenes supported those with fortunate long tenures in Louisiana's campus ministry is Robert L. Lee, retired executive secretary of the Louisiana Baptist Convention. Lee labored for almost four decades to assure the success of that state's Baptist Student Union (BSU) program.

He also was BSU's advocate meeting with executive secretaries from other states across the convention. Without him, today's Louisiana pulpits and those beyond would not be so vastly filled by people who were products of Baptist Student Unions across the Bayou State. We ought not to leave out those Louisiana "BSUers" who are now serving Christ around the world. All campus ministers over the Southern Baptist Convention are in his debt. This tribute is small compared to his labor for Baptist student work.

All of my readers made their peculiar contribution for which I am grateful. C. William Junker of Nashville, retired editor of materials at the Baptist Home Mission Board, did yeoman's service in editing the manuscript and writing the foreword. He, in many ways, could be the silent coauthor of this work. Now I know why writers express appreciation to editors.

The Robert Gowdys—Anne especially—English professors at two universities in Knoxville, Tennessee, did the Herculean task of correcting atrocious grammar and syntax. Wasn't it Oscar Wilde who once described Paul's prose style as one of the principal arguments against Christianity?

G. Avery Lee of New Orleans and Glen Edwards of San Angelo, Texas, made their unique contributions—both from the perspective of collegiate pastors. Walter Shurden, noted Baptist historian, deserves a nod of appreciation for his encouragement.

Walker L. Knight, a golf partner, taught me to use a new computer when the old one died. All this delayed the manuscript for months. Knight also contributed his mission expertise to this volume, especially the section on the Jesus people, and acted as my "agent" in clearing the multitudinous details of publishing. He, in

11

my life, represents a genuine follower of the gentle Jesus, and one of few prophets among Southern Baptists.

I am deeply indebted to the people at Providence House for their yeoman's work on the manuscript, especially Elaine Kernea, Joanne Jaworski, and Charles Deweese.

To Esther, my esteemed wife of fifty years, I am reminded of the two lovers singing as the showers dripped on the roof of the gazebo in *The Sound of Music:* "Here I stand loving you. Somewhere in my youth and childhood, I must have done something good." Thank you for your criticism, encouragement, patience, and persevering. You are God's interfering presence when I rush headlong down the many paths of sanctity.

With sacred hope, may this volume help those in universities and seminaries as they study, collegiate ministers who strive each Lord's day to express God's word to academicians, in the lives of mature campus ministers, and those contemplating God's will in doing this honorable task.

To those who see your thoughts and ideas in these pages, all I can say is a word of appreciation for enriching my life and that of Baptist campus ministry. However, I take full responsibility for the contents of this work.

INTRODUCTION

Continuing Education on an Anniversary

Socrates said the unexamined life was not worth living. If that statement is true, the unexamined past makes the unknown future of any movement questionable.

Southern Baptists' Christian program to students on university campuses celebrates its diamond anniversary in 1997. One can argue that this program provides more results with less expenditure of money per capita than many others this denomination has fostered. Southern Baptists owe an incalculable debt to the Baptist Student Union (BSU).

BSU was born among Southern Baptists on January 1, 1922, in Memphis, Tennessee. Frank Hartwell Leavell Sr. led this communion of Baptists until he died of heart failure in 1949. As Claude Broach observed, "It was an humble beginning—one room, two desks, a typewriter, a stenographer, an executive-secretary, and a dream."[1]

For seventy-five years the national organization has been the incubator for huge numbers of local church and other staff ministers, missionaries at home and around the globe, and denominational agency personnel. How can one count the young people who, through Jesus the Christ and Baptist Student Union, became committed laypersons, teachers and leaders in Sunday Schools, and members of church boards locally, in states, and in the denomination? One should recall the multitude of scientists, business men and women, educators, government officials, and others, who "played out" the Christian faith in their vocational pursuits. Neither should it be forgotten how many students who first met at a BSU function fell in love, married, and provided children for Christian homes. ("BSUers" never die; they just marry and multiply.) This group became the leaven that turned to many and various loaves for Southern Baptists.

Woman's Missionary Union (WMU) is another group that has done much for Baptist young people and world missions. Any student who lost the opportunity of being involved in either WMU in churches or BSU on campuses is poorer for the lack of missionary education. In racing parlance, it is a dead heat between these groups in influencing people to become a part of the communion's global missions. BSU and WMU took seriously what one author insisted, "In any case, when the church is looking for a mission field, it need not look beyond the nearest campus."[2]

13

If campus ministers of the 1990s are people who understand their unique calling, one thing is obvious: they must be willing to travel the road of continuing education. One of the roads to be pursued is the map of the past. How did campus ministry get to where it is today? Who were those who provided the vision for God's work on campus that extended around the world? What changes have been made in this organization as the world of the twentieth century has changed?

G. Avery Lee was my campus minister beginning in 1941. I came to Louisiana State University (LSU) as a lonely lad from a family broken by my mother's death. I was struggling with my faith, particularly with the group called church. What I had seen in the lives of some of the congregates of north Louisiana caused me serious doubt that Christianity was the water that flowed through every arena of life.

At LSU somehow I wandered over to the student center of the BSU. There I found a young minister, Avery Lee, who had just returned from Yale University with his vivacious bride, Ann. Little did I realize these two were going to be a part of my life for a half-century. Avery was intelligent and optimistic. If he had decided to go after Moby Dick, he would have taken Tabasco and tartar sauces!

I commented years later after Ann had died of facial basal/squamous carcinoma:

> Influence is the art of a person's life being projected into others without either realizing it. Now I know that whatever I have become is due to her—and Avery's—influence. At times I must have exasperated her, but she could see potential and knew how to hew God's possibilities from human probabilities.

> Human probabilities in my life have been many; God's possibilities require something of the miraculous. Even at this hour my confession would have overtones of Christian skepticism. Compound skepticism with a physical handicap, and anyone would not have to take long to figure the slim chance of probability becoming possibility.[3]

This discussion about a campus minister and one of his students may seem like an interlude in the midst of a volume whose polemic argues that BSU is an extension of the Great Commission. However, what greater mission cause is there than to provide a haven for the refugees of the world? This refugee, enabled through being a part of the LSU Baptist family of God, also regained a place in the family of humankind. BSU, even on the local campus, is a mission enterprise.

Another thesis will be argued: the American missionary movement began, basically, as a student phenomenon. Twenty years after my university days, Avery Lee and I were colleagues in New Orleans. At a local Baptist associational meeting, he spoke on the subject of "How the Churches Benefit from the Baptist Student Union":

> In 1534 Ignatius Loyola and John Calvin were contemporaries enrolled at the University of Paris. From these students came the founder of the Society of Jesuits and one of the leaders of the Protestant Reformation. In 1730 John

and Charles Wesley were students at Oxford. Although the largest group that ever met with them was twenty-nine, from it came the denomination called Methodists.

Most student groups have been formed in opposition not only to the campus authorities but also to the church. The Wesleyan group met such opposition. One Oxford professor said, "We yet will have done with this Godly group." The Haystack Prayer Meeting of 1806, consisting of five students, launched the foreign mission movement in America. Young people in general and students in particular have opened new vistas for the Christian faith and most of the time in opposition to their adult counterparts.[4]

THREE PERSPECTIVES ON THE CAMPUS MISSION ENTERPRISE

The initial part of this book will contain the discussion about how churches abdicated missionary involvement in the nineteenth century. (That would not be the last time they would give issues to student programs when churches did not want involvement.) One reference emphasized the place of students in missionary endeavor: Kenneth Scott Latourette, a noted world mission scholar alleged, "It was from the Haystack Prayer Meeting that the foreign missionary movement of the churches of the United States had an *initial* [italics mine] main impulse."[5]

The second perspective to be explored is whether or not the Baptist student movement has evolved from its original focus of denominational conservation, devotional emphasis, and a counteraction to subchristian campus activities into a profound proclamation of the Christian faith to the academic community. Two perplexities keep this question valid: First, Southern Baptists have focused on evangelism and missions, which left little time for other faith questions in the academy. However, students of campus work should recall that the neglect of evangelism in Baptist student programs during the 1960s may have created a vacuum for nondenominational programs such as Campus Crusade for Christ. The second perplexity was the need to keep close to past practices of Southern Baptists, which favored "spiritual" over "academic" pursuits. W. T. Conner pondered this problem with regard to Southern Baptist seminaries. Walter Thomas Conner was perhaps the leading conservative theologian in the nation as professor of theology at Southwestern Baptist Theological Seminary in Fort Worth, Texas, from 1910 until the middle 1940s. He lent credence to the question of narrow spirituality as it affects the faith academically. Stewart Newman, a faculty colleague of Conner's, wrote the great thinker's biography. He observed Conner's concern about the school's academic character:

> The mood and spirit of its church constituency affected the academic character. . . . From its earliest years the distance from its classroom to its altar was negligible.

Those who guided the seminary viewed the matter from deep within the religious perspective. To preclude a development that would shift the emphasis toward the academic, they weighed the balance heavily in the opposite direction. They planned it so as to make its chief interest spiritual, thereby seeking to make sure that its operation would never be "lost" to the denomination.[6]

This theme will flow through the manuscript.

A third perspective is this: Do those who are now in leadership positions know how to do campus ministry in this era? Are they still grasping the old ways? Do Baptists refuse to assimilate Christian student programs that can focus the unchanging message of good news for a 1990s type of world?

Ralph C. Dunlop, chaplain at Northwestern University, argued long ago in the 1960s:

We used to think we knew quite well how "to do student work." We don't anymore! The techniques of group work and the programmatic approach seemed once to work fairly well. Not any more. This makes our work infinitely more difficult and frustrating. Advisory board . . . on higher education may be demanding that the director of the Wesley Foundation "produce results" by which they mean "get more students involved." But too often more students do not come. . . . We may be in for leaner days so far as student response to what the Wesley Foundation offers is concerned.[7]

Dunlop was a prophet. Mainline denominations, except Southern Baptists and Roman Catholics, began to change their programs and philosophies. Yet, students who should have been a part of those mainline communions did not come.

Then, ecumenicists reasoned, mainline Protestants should band together and save the university. That was the tragic philosophical error of the 1960s for ecumenical campus ministries. God does not work in organizations of brick and mortar; he works in the lives of individuals. Perhaps as early as the middle 1970s, Baptist leaders involved with students should have been pondering the same question others had asked in the middle 1960s. Are BSU programs sufficiently relevant for this day and time?

Two influential factors help to determine the answer to this question. The first came in the middle seventies when the culture of narcissism swept the nation, including universities and Baptist Student Unions. The other came in 1979 when fundamentalists began the takeover of the Southern Baptist Convention (SBC) that coincided with the nation's conservative resurgence. The narcissism factor substantially ended the BSU era described as one that expanded like kudzu. (Kudzu was supposed to save the awful erosion of southern soil; instead, it proved to be so fast-growing there was no way to contain it. Consequently, the South has been inundated with this plant.) About 1976—following the aborted Jesus

Movement—the "me-generation" mentality polluted the actions of students, even those who called themselves Christians.

An enormous amount of literature has been written on this narcissistic theme.[8] "What is in it for me?" became the hue and cry not only of young people but also the general populace. The prestigious master's of business administration became the "only" degree in the minds of a majority of students whose goal was to earn "big bucks" in a hurry. Liberal arts education gave way to professional degrees. Allan Bloom called this era the closing of the American mind. Jobs were "out there" if the grades were "in here." Nevertheless, by the end of the 1980s, America was experiencing financial recession.

This "me generation," which included enormous numbers of students in Baptist Student Unions, affected its program. Unfortunately, instead of challenging students on the ministry levels of the gospel, Baptist leaders also turned inward. Programs began to develop such as Discipleship and Masterlife studies that— though needful—met only the person-to-God relationship of the gospel. Students of the 1980s were an introspective lot.

During this same period, as has been noted, fundamentalists began the crusade to take over SBC. This is historical fact. However, it is not the purpose of this volume to interpret what now has become known simply as "the controversy." Excellent books are available on this subject; perhaps enough have been written.[9] Yet, undeniably, the controversy has affected Southern Baptist campus ministry as it has every entity of Southern Baptist life. This phenomenon will be expanded in chapter 9 as "Living in a Smaller Biosphere."

The severest limitation to this study is the author's personal philosophy as to the development of Southern Baptists' student program. I write from my preconceptions, prejudices, and other personal limitations. Reprimands have already been expressed by friends—I have not needed to turn elsewhere—that we should not expect those who serve today in this particular vocation to be clones of those who have gone before.

This book is dedicated to those who "professionalized" Southern Baptist campus ministry. They were the second generation of Baptist student workers, but were the first generation who spent entire lives on local campuses having pursued the calling for "the unusual." They survived being rejected outside the confines of academe, though accepted within. This generation of campus ministers reminded me of that almost hidden portion of a verse in the Westminster Abbey of Faith, Heb. 11. As was written of the prophets of old, these are people "of whom the world [is] not worthy" (Heb. 11:35, RSV). They accepted as a great part of their biblical belief the challenge of both the threat and the promise of knowledge.

John Cantelon, a Presbyterian and then chaplain at the University of Southern California, expressed this same vision when he contended that in spite of the two-edged sword of knowledge—threat and promise—profound biblical faith still has the power to transform people in the university setting:

It is fascinating to read in the first book of the Bible how the tree of knowledge is presented as a threat to man. Genesis would seem to tell us that when man grasps knowledge for his own purposes, when man uses this knowledge in a way in which he is not responsible either to God or to his neighbor, this knowledge becomes the source of his damnation.

But at the other end of the Bible in The Revelation, there is the tree of knowledge again, but here its leaves are used for the healing of the nations. This would seem to tell us that knowledge is always two-edged—full of threat as well as promise—but that knowledge for redeemed man has a healing quality that is absolutely essential.[10]

Thirty years ago that statement was true. It is true today. Life is somewhere between the threat of Genesis and the eschatological perspective of The Revelation. A friend titled his memoirs *Living in the Meantime*. Both he and Cantelon provided the thinking for the challenge of campus ministry as time speeds into the twenty-first century. As long as knowledge remains two-edged, new concepts for campus ministries are requirement courses for new campus ministers and continuing education for students of student work.

The promise of knowledge is eternal. Jesus said to Nicodemus in the dark of night, "The wind blows where it chooses, and you hear the sound of it, but you do not know where it comes from or where it goes. So it is with everyone who is born of the Spirit" (John 3:8, NRSV).

Donald G. Shockley, a former chaplain at Atlanta's Emory University, closes his excellent book, *Campus Ministry—The Church Beyond Itself*, with a challenge for all involved in campus ministry in the last decade of the twentieth century. His awareness of history as a link to the present is apparent:

"We are the beneficiaries of the courage and work of . . . earlier generations who created the phenomenon . . . called campus ministry. Having gleaned so much from their labors, we must now take our turn at the task of sowing fresh seeds."[11]

Listen! Do campus religious leaders hear the holy wind today as they heard it surrounding young academicians for seventy-five years whispering "Follow me! I will make you fishers of men"? Listen!

"Remember Thy Creator in the Days of Thy Youth"
(Early American Student Movements)

The introduction suggested that European youth blazed the beginning of student movements: Loyola spawned the Jesuits at the University of Paris, while in Britain the Wesleys, as students, were to become the founders of Methodism. Flavored by American students, their programs launched the first foreign mission movement.

Referring particularly to the student Haystack Prayer meeting of August 1806 on a mountainside near Williams College, mission scholar Kenneth Scott Latourette argued that it was from this meeting that the foreign missionary movement of the churches of the United States had an initial impulse.[1]

CHURCH: WHERE WERE YOU?

What was the colonial church doing when it ignored the Great Commission? America's first student of student movements, Yale professor Clarence Shedd, suggested, "The American church was so completely occupied with its . . . missionary service to the Indians that the world-wide implications of Jesus' missionary commands had little place in the counsels of its leaders."[2]

Others were not so kind. One author, commenting about this same issue, proposed ". . . whether this was for lack of opportunity and means, indifference, wars, eschatology, or doctrine is not known. For instance, Wittenberg's theological faculty showed little interest in missions on the grounds that countries still languishing in heathenism were obviously under the judgment of God."[3] Similar-type church groups—some Baptists included—would express the same idea crudely: "If God wants the heathen saved, he, without help, will do it!"

As the years rolled by, another "doctrine" would not go away. Southern Baptists were plagued in the nineteenth century with Landmark theology. This "doctrine" affected the way missions were done. Missionaries, according to this position, could come from only local churches. J. M. Pendleton and J. R. Graves originated Landmarkism. It remained just a doctrinal position and never became denominationalized by Southern Baptists, although its shadow has followed them through the years. One can draw an arc from Kentucky, over western Tennessee, through Arkansas, northwest Louisiana, and northern Texas and see the effects of the shadow. "Local church" doctrine of that group did pour into the theology of SBC churches. This group deterred Baptist mission endeavors during the latter nineteenth century.

Few missionaries come from local Landmark churches; they do not have the financial ability to back their local church doctrine. Therefore, agencies the size of SBC's home and foreign mission boards, with funds from more than thirty thousand churches, can service thousands as a part of missionary endeavor.

A final matter should be considered. The colonial church may have been consumed with education. According to Donald Shockley, former chaplain at Emory University, it is wrong to assume that colonial colleges were formed for the *sole* purpose of educating the clergy:

> In founding the first institution of higher education [Harvard] . . . the colonists were acting on their hope of creating an exemplary society, a new order in which the intention of God for human life will prevail. Their mission was to train what might be thought of as morally intelligent leadership for the whole community, not just for the church. As a democratic form of national government emerged, it became all the more critical to be concerned about what people in general valued. Without an educated citizenry, democracy would fail. At the time, it seemed rather clear that familiarity with a distinct body of literature drawn from the classics, the Bible, Christian theology, and moral philosophy would meet the aims of education. All this, of course, was to take place in an ethos of Protestant piety.[4]

Whatever anyone may ask about the lack of missionary emphasis in colonial churches of a fledgling nation, the fact is the missionary enterprise happened. Students prayed and acted. They launched America's foreign missionary work.

EIGHTEENTH- AND NINETEENTH-CENTURY STUDENT SOCIETIES

For two centuries churches and education followed geographical movements across the nation. Generally the church and particularly Calvinists based their government on alleged biblical principles. The purpose of colonial education in New England was clearly expressed in Yale University's charter. It proposed that "students be so educated that they might be fitted for publick [sic] employment both in Church and Civil State."[5] During these two centuries the church remained the controlling influence in education, ministering to the religious needs of students through its own schools and colleges.

However, the question still arises: Why did student religious societies begin if the church was ministering to students' needs? Historians are silent as to whether church opposition, apathy, or preoccupation elsewhere caused those groups to develop. Charles Barnes, retired University of Alabama campus minister, has suggested in his doctoral dissertation that these societies were secret ones. Barnes also stated that the minutes of the meetings were in "script" so that others would not know what they contained.[6] Whatever the reason, student groups were originally separate entities from the church.

Purposes

Four purposes emerged from these groups and remained relatively constant during the years from 1700 through 1850:

1. An opportunity for worship experiences, nurturing the devotional life, and Christian fellowship.
2. Mutual watchfulness over the moral conduct of its members.
3. Combating of the atmosphere of colleges, thought to be evil institutions.
4. Intellectual elements were a definite part of the program.[7]

Informal worship groups filled a need the church seemingly did not. Whatever the reasons were, Sunday evenings became a time of worship. Students, at their own initiative, prayed together, "repeated" a sermon, and concluded by singing a psalm.

The second purpose is indicative of the early Baptist Student Unions. They watched over one another to not unkindly divulge one another's infirmities, yet *lovingly* inform each of the other's faults. This reminds one of unsigned letters of reprimand by church members who always close them, "Lovingly, in Jesus' name."

The third purpose also reflects early BSU days. The university was thought "godless." These early groups thought nothing could remedy the situation.[8] Consequently, students gathered secretly not only to combat the evils of collegiate living but also to escape the ridicule of fellow collegians. Shedd vividly described this problem:

> These movements struggled for ascendancy, particularly at Williams College, although it was true among students everywhere. Infidelity became rampant even to the point of persecution. Ridicule and abuse were heaped upon any students who showed signs of Christianity. During the first seven years of the existence of Williams [in which ninety-three graduated in six classes] there were but five professors of religion.[9]

There is no evidence of ridicule of early BSU members, but through the leaders of this embryonic organization, campus living gave an undercurrent feeling of living in a pagan country. For example, dances on campus were always accompanied by simultaneous activities at the BSU so that Christians could have their "spiritual temperatures" checked—at least, Baptist Christians could.

Incidentally, times and mores do change. In December 1994 the University of Tennessee BSU hosted a Christmas banquet. The food was donated; funds from the price of the students' tickets were in turn donated to community charities. After the dinner, a *dance* was held in which lessons for ballroom dancing were taught.[10]

Interestingly, the ballroom dancing lessons were not taught at the Baptist student center. (November 23, 1996, the *Atlanta Constitution* headlined an article about dancing on a Baptist campus "Baylor Boogies.")

The fourth purpose for these early groups was the most sound, a purpose that has permeated all religious groups including BSU through the years. (There may be some question today as to whether or not this purpose is paramount as it was before the 1980s.) This was intellectual element: to confront moral and ethical issues.

Clarence Shedd in his monumental work *Two Centuries of Christian Student Movements* explained three great issues that occupied seventeenth century collegians: slavery, temperance, and the "menace of Unitarianism." Other interesting discussions debated seem surprisingly modern: Should divorce be granted? Is lying justifiable? Is it fornication to lie with one's sweetheart after engagement but before marriage? Students were sound in theological views, yet liberal on many of the ethical questions of the day.

Moving quickly to 1924, one finds the discussions similar. Jane Young Poster wrote about the Baptist Student Union Convention in South Carolina that year. In her book *Reckless for Christ,* a quotation from the state's Baptist paper stated the following:

> There were open conferences where students debated campus problems. Some of these were: "Do students on your campus hobo [hitchhike] on trains? Is this stealing?" "How about smoking, cursing, drinking?" and "How long since you led a soul to Christ?" . . . They pledged to carry out their faith in a "reckless" manner in order to make a difference on campus.[11]

The original purposes of these early American student groups were the foundation for the existence of student religious organizations for the first 150 years on the early American educational scene. These societies were indigenous to the religious and educational life of American colleges; they were interdenominational in outlook and composition; and perhaps most important, they were student movements—there is no evidence of adult leadership.

Result—World Missions

The significant result of student groups was the launching of world missions from American shores. History assumes that one student, Samuel J. Mills Jr. (1783–1818), was instrumental in the beginning of this movement. One event was its impetus—the Haystack Prayer Meeting—August 1806.[12]

Mills was the son of a congregational minister and was reared in a godly home. His mother said of him, "I have consecrated this child to the service of God as a missionary."[13] This was a remarkable statement since missionary interest was practically non-existent in churches of that day.

In 1806 Mills enrolled at Williams College and joined other students who were products of the Great Awakening. It was Mills's practice, with others, to spend two afternoons a week in prayer. One afternoon the students were caught in a rainstorm and sought refuge under a haystack. The focus of prayer that day was for the awakening of foreign mission emphasis. Four years later, six men sailed to Calcutta as missionaries.

Three effective student religious groups came from this era. They were the Moral Society of Yale, Adelphoi Theologia of Harvard, and the Andover Society. The first two were concerned with Christian witnessing to all people—particularly the "heathen." *Heathen* was a synonym for those in "far away places with strange sounding names." The Andover Society was the *result* of foreign mission activity. Support of missionaries who had already gone was carried on by this group. It started at Andover Seminary and spread throughout New England's campuses.

Shedd concluded this century and a half of student religious movements:

> One stream is found in the gradual growth of . . . Christian student societies. The second stream was started by the group which led directly from Williams College to the Young Men's Christian Association . . . the whole history of the Christian church tends to show the clearest vision with regard to things near at hand had generally come from youth who, taking seriously Jesus' way of life and His attitude toward God and man, had been restless until in some effective way they were enabled to share their views with every living human being.[14]

THE INTERCOLLEGIATE YOUNG MEN'S CHRISTIAN ASSOCIATION

The first Young Men's Christian Association (YMCA) was not collegiate in nature. Only the wildest dreams of George Wilson and his fellow clerks could have imagined the ultimate significance of their London dry goods store activity. Each morning they met for prayer and Bible study. By coincidence a college student heard of this meeting and wrote to friends in America describing the program. The essence of it became the YMCA in America.

The first YMCA, formed in Boston on December 22, 1851, was designed for destitute men. The association was clearly a product of city conditions. Its methods alleviated the problems of city youth; therefore, many of its adult leaders refused to think it was adaptable for student needs.

A universal trait of students is apparent by their reaction to adult leadership—they could always prove them wrong. In spite of what adults thought, two YMCA affiliates were organized, one on the campus of the University of Michigan and one on the University of Virginia campus.

Howard Hopkins, a YMCA historian, noted that previous societies soon became YMCA affiliates:

Many older student religious societies metamorphosed into YMCA affiliates. The academic year 1864-65 . . . saw the transformation of the Judson Association of Missionary Inquirey [sic] at the University of Rochester into a student YMCA that was to be widely influential—a development characteristic of this era.[15]

By 1877 a national organization had been formed and Luther D. Wishard was elected the first "student secretary" in the nation. Frank Leavell, the first Southwide Baptist student secretary would, in 1922, copy this same terminology. When there was a question about this he would say, "If national cabinet members can be called 'secretaries' so can Baptist student leaders."

The same year, 1877, the first national YMCA convention met in Louisville, Kentucky. Without any preliminary studies, except those done spasmodically over the past decade, Wishard was invited to present to the Louisville conference his philosophical proposals concerning this embryonic organization. Not framed in formal or academic language, he proposed the following:

1. The importance of seeking the salvation of students for their own sake and their influence as educated men.
2. The importance of securing salvation while in college.
3. The value of unity and prayer. The success of this work depended upon:
    1) Diligent study of the Word of God.
    2) Prayer
    3) Personal work
    4) Efficient organization[16]

No evidence exists that this group's philosophy changed during the next three decades. YMCA prospered, grew in numbers, and became an international organization. Men such as Wishard and his successor, John R. Mott, brought a strong evangelistic flavor to this design. Mott gave his life and created his international fame by these principles.

Young movements are generally synonymous with the personalities who first lead them. The temptation—rightly so—is to eulogize individuals like Wishard and Mott. The fact remains that these two men and YMCA have been synonymous. (It was likewise with Leavell's launching Southern Baptists' student work program.) Sabin Landry, former professor of campus ministries at the Southern Baptist Theological Seminary, in paying tribute to the founders of YMCA, declared: "they chartered the course, established the policies, and developed the techniques. Those who came after adopted and utilized as their own much of what had been tried and proven in previous years as a part of the program of this organization."[17]

This program involved national leadership, student initiative, student secretaries, and association buildings—which found significance in other church-related programs, including BSU. For nearly a half-century, YMCA interpreted the Christian faith to members of the academic community.

YMCA's Changing Philosophy

During the first twenty years of this century, several contingencies arose almost simultaneously so that trying to determine which contingency affected the other is difficult (i.e., the chicken or egg theory). The church was wakening to its responsibility in the academic community, and conflicts rose within churches' denominational leadership as to the effectiveness of YMCA.

There were valid reasons for the churches' concern because during the decade from 1910 to 1920 YMCA was departing radically from its original foundations. "New realism"—a new way of expressing itself—was apparent in the urgings of new leadership:

1. A new realism about the nature of the world and the Christian message.
2. A new realism abut the Christian message and the social order.
3. A new realism about YMCA and war.
4. A new realism concerning Christian internationalism.
5. A new realism about YMCA and the changing educational scene.[18]

Several questions are pertinent. Did the interest of denominations begin to take the spotlight from YMCA, thereby forcing interdenominationalism to seek a new *raison d'être?* Did the theological issues of the day cause YMCA to emphasize the "social gospel"? If so, they forgot their history of seeking persons who needed an encounter with God. Did World War I and Mott's simultaneous retirement give reason for YMCA affiliates to seek new directions? A present-day question exists as well: There were Young Women's Christian Associations—did they assume a secondary role to that which was a "men's only" club?

To say the changes in YMCA philosophy caused concern in denominationally minded churches is fair. Consequently, "new realism" hastened all denominations' interest in their students' spiritual well-being.

CONCLUSION: AN AWAKENING OF THE CHURCH

At the time YMCA was struggling with new ways to express the Christian faith, the church was waking to responsibility for students and their Christian lives. This brought conflict. Conflict arose because of the continuing strength and usefulness of the student associations and because they were widely accepted by many churches and universities. Local church ministers and lay leaders were products of YMCA. They did not want to see the organization that gave them spiritual nurture challenged.

Another conflict within the church was the feeling that by supporting a strong denominational witness at state-supported universities, church-supported schools would be destroyed. One Presbyterian cleric commented: "it must be admitted . . . that whatever antagonism to this work is being encountered finds its home in the denominational college. It is scarcely to be wondered at when distinguished educators boldly prophesy that the [state] University has rung the death knell of the Church College."[19]

Southern Baptists and their leaders were going to have to deal with this problem of developing their program on the state university level. Broach acutely observed the situation:

> Paradoxically, it was quite often true that B. S. U. has hard sledding in the denomination's schools. Patiently, tactfully, Frank [Leavell] sought to meet this problem and understand it. The crux of the matter seemed to lie in the fact that some administrators were prone to assume that since the school was Christian in name and motive, no special emphasis on spiritual growth was needed beyond that which was supplied through the normal channels of campus life.[20]

To a certain extent, the assumption by Baptist school administrators is true; however, a larger question needs debating. How *Christian* are Baptist schools? Do these schools affect *every* student as Christ's child? If so, there is no need for campus religious groups on denominational school campuses. If not, Baptist Student Unions are an ongoing need. The paradox between BSU and Baptists' philosophy of Christian education will have its answer through reasonable people who understand what each group, from different perspectives, is trying to do. The debate continues.

Joseph W. Cochran, the secretary of the Board of Education of the Presbyterian Church, was the first and strongest voice in the years of YMCA changes. He sought to bring his church's attention to providing a basis for a Christian witness in the academic community. He felt deeply that YMCA establishments could not and were not ministering to the spiritual needs of university students. He emphasized in an article in *Religious Education*:

> The Christian Associations have wrought a notable work in our colleges and universities. . . . While church leaders have been expending their energies upon denominational problems in education, the Christian Associations entered church and state institutions alike. The question is often raised whether the Associations are real extensions of the church or actually separate denominations supported by the church. . . . They are charged with a policy that tends to wean the student away from his old time religious affiliations; when he returns to the world of affairs, he finds himself detached from any organized form of religion.[21]

Conflict with YMCA philosophically, as well as exhortation from leaders of various communions for the establishment of their own student movements, was the foundation for denominational campus ministry.

Conservation for a Denomination
(Baptist Student Union Origins)

As the morning sun rose on the first two decades of the twentieth century, two primary factors were the incentives for the rise of denominational student movements. Not only had conflict arisen over YMCA programs, but also most denominations were giving serious thought to their own programs of student work. Here was a great mission field, as observed by Clarence Shedd:

> With the turn of the century pioneering began in earnest. A few denominational leaders were beginning to see the importance of developing church-centered student programs . . . for their students in state universities. For this work there were no supporting constituencies, no inherited methods of procedure, no precedents except the work of the Christian Associations.[1]

SOUTHERN BAPTISTS' SCATTERED EFFORTS FOR STUDENT MINISTRY

The educational secretary of the Southern Baptist Foreign Mission Board (FMB), as early as 1908, visited and lectured at Baptist colleges throughout the South for the purpose of securing personnel. Woman's Missionary Union (WMU), by 1910, was attempting to reach young women on the campuses of the South to conserve them for their own organizations—a vital part of Baptist churches. In addition, the Baptist Sunday School Board was working among collegians before 1920. The desire of B. W. Spillman, the board's educational director, was to establish "teacher training classes" for maintaining doctrinal "purity" among Baptist students. The 1918 annual SBC report showed Spillman's broader emphasis: "He is keeping alive interest in Sunday School as an institution in the schools and colleges, and *especially* those under state control."[2]

Another scattered effort for students was the Baptist Student Missionary Movement. Charles Ball, a missions professor at Fort Worth's Southwestern Seminary, felt a need for an organization to replenish the mission fields. In a master's degree thesis at Southwestern, Andrew Allen wrote about the beginnings of and apparent opposition to this movement:

They were conscious that there was much opposition to the idea. Many felt this effort would replace the Student Volunteer Movement [an ecumenical organization], and they were indignant about it. . . . It had been the only organization that ministered to their Christian needs in college, and they were jealous for its success. It was dangerous simply because it expressed a new idea and method. Many Baptist leaders and students openly opposed the idea of a new Baptist organization.[3]

The idea of this organization was soon aborted. It did heighten the need and the turning to favor for Baptist student work. Hight C. Moore, a North Carolina state Baptist editor, was insistent that this work was imperative. Other leaders throughout the convention took up the hue and cry, causing Sabin Landry to comment, "Although the Baptist Student Missionary Movement was comparatively short-lived, it attracted considerable attention and thereby helped to keep before Southern Baptists the greater need for work among their college and university students."

LOCAL CHURCHES' ATTEMPTS AT BSU BEGINNINGS

In addition to the activities of SBC and the Baptist Student Missionary Movement, two states were revealing interest in Baptist students prior to and in the early 1920s. Historians never agree on where or exactly when BSU began. Shedd suggested that the distinctiveness of this group was its beginning in local churches. Leavell supported Shedd's observation. The University Baptist Church of Austin, Texas, has been an illustration of the slow metamorphosis of student work in a local church. G. Avery Lee's history of St. Charles Avenue Baptist in New Orleans included the following insertion from church minutes:

In December of 1920 St. Charles Avenue Baptist [church] in New Orleans requested the Executive Board of the Louisiana Baptist Convention to share in financial arrangements for a "college bred" young man to work with the students of Tulane University, Newcomb College and other New Orleans institutions of higher learning.[4]

There is no indication that this church's request was granted. However, it paints a picture of faint beginnings that would blossom into untold blessings for thousands of students coming into and leaving from the Crescent City in future decades. St. Charles Church built one of the first Baptist student centers on their property that was only four blocks from Tulane, Newcomb, and Loyola campuses. Even Leavell, however, would say these examples were not typical, so state conventions began to synchronize the scattered efforts of different groups.

Two State Conventions Work with Students

The 1919 convention annuals of both Texas and Mississippi show the interest the conventions had in student work. However, Texas was the first state to take concrete action; the following resolution was passed by the general convention in that year:

> BE IT RESOLVED: 1. That the executive board of the convention select and direct one of the strongest and most capable men to be secured as Baptist Student Secretary for students of Texas. That this man give his entire time among the Baptist students of Texas emphasizing Baptist principles, interpreting Baptist life, creating and sustaining Baptist loyalty, enlisting and crystallizing a denominational spirit, virile, consecrated, and active, and that shall express itself through the local churches where students hold membership.
>
> 2. That the Sunday School Board be asked to cooperate in the support of this secretary and that it be understood that this man represents the whole Baptist program rather than any special department.[5]

This lengthy quotation is important. The wording of this resolution became almost the exact philosophy of Frank Leavell upon his election as the first Southwide student secretary in 1922. Interestingly, his first trip after assuming the new position was to Texas to see how the work progressed under the conditions outlined by that general convention.

The Texas program was quickly implemented. J. P. Boone became the convention's (and SBC's) first state secretary of student work. He immediately arranged a student conference at Palacios, Texas, to take place during the summer of 1920. The purpose was to start an organization to promote the religious interests of students in all institutions. The conferees chose the name *Baptist Student Union*.

Mississippi Baptists, in 1919 at their annual state convention, voted to secure "a Baptist student field man" to work with that state's students. However, the position was not implemented until 1924. Interesting differences developed in the two states' emphases.

The Texas resolution had strong positive tones. They included a singular Baptist viewpoint with overtones of developing deep, consecrated spiritual lives by students in academic communities. The Mississippi resolution contained the same significant wording, but had a defensive tone:

> In view of the fact that a quiet but insidious propaganda has been launched to undenominationalize Christianity and in view of the fact that hundreds of our boys are in agricultural schools and state colleges where inadequate effort is made to hold them to their churches, we therefore recommend that a Baptist student field man be appointed who is to work under the direction of the secretary of the State Mission Board, his duties to be defined by the board.[6]

These two state resolutions became the foundational philosophy for Baptist student work. The conservation of youth for their denomination was the primary concern of those in SBC, the states, and local churches. Born out of the fear of the larger ecumenical movement, a distinctive denominational enterprise began on local and state levels.

THE INTER-BOARD COMMISSION, 1921–1928

The Inter-Board Commission on Student Religious Activity was the result of the 1920 SBC asking for cooperative effort in the interest of students throughout the South. The convention further approved that the work be done through a committee comprised of the corresponding secretaries of the Foreign Mission, Home Mission, Sunday School, and Education Boards. A member from WMU was added. In 1921 SBC approved the action of the commission and the employment of Frank Hartwell Leavell Sr. as executive secretary. Memphis was selected as the commission's headquarters; none of the other agencies were located there.

Concerning those initial days, Leavell wrote in the last year of his life, "It was an humble beginning—one room, two desks, a typewriter, a stenographer, and an executive secretary. *But*, it was undergirded by a tremendous conviction on the part of a few, and by the prayers and the resources of the great Southern Baptist Convention."[7]

By 1924 discussion developed among convention leaders concerning the control of the Inter-Board Commission. This was only the first time discussion of this nature would arise about the place of Baptists' campus ministry program; its *place in what agency* has been a topic of debate through much of its lifetime. Some were thinking that the developing program of student work should be assigned to what is known today as the Education Commission. (Under the restructuring of the SBC in 1997, this commission will no longer exist.)

In a letter dated May 5, 1924, to twelve leading educators and pastors, Leavell informed them:

> The Committee on Correlation and Unification at present is recommending that our work be transferred to the Education Board. That committee is to meet again and I am to appear before it, upon instructions of the Inter-Board Commission, to protest and plead for the continuation of our present plan of approach.[8]

The letter pled for other voices of leadership to be added to his. The matter would be brought before the forthcoming convention. Some of the reasons he gave for the continuation of the commission were as follows:

- The Inter-Board Commission had voted in its last two meetings for its continuance.

- Only three years earlier the convention had deliberately created the commission because it felt this was the only way the task could be accomplished.

- The essence of the inter-board idea was unification.

- Work that would be committed to one board would mean the other boards would have no voice in the student program.

- The program has started very successfully under the commission idea and should not be disturbed.

- A very significant phase of this question which is extremely difficult for the rank and file to grasp is the fact that our work is a missionary task and not an educational task. The Education Board is founded upon the basis of an academic and curriculum development. Our work touches neither the curriculum nor the academic work of the institutions. It is a missionary task in which the Sunday School Board and the distinctly Mission Boards rather than the Education Board are directly, fundamentally and vitally interested. It is a missionary task with an educational constituency.[9]

- The last reason for the continuation of the commission was the most significant. Leavell saved it to distinguish between the philosophy of student work and that of the now-called Education Commission:

  > Although the idea of the Education Board assuming the work faded, the issue concerning the Inter-Board Commission continued. In spite of Leavell's efforts, along with the commission's opposition, the annual convention of 1928 voted to transfer the work to the Sunday School Board.

Certainly the secretary's reasons had merit, but there was another factor involved. The Sunday School Board had been paying half of the expense of the commission, plus absorbing the losses on publishing the *Baptist Student* magazine. Finally, in spite of Leavell's opposition, the 1928 annual convention decided to transfer the Inter-Board Commission to the Sunday School Board. They asked this agency to assume the financial obligations of what would become the Southwide Student Department. Despite what seemed to be good student work philosophy to maintain an multiboard agency, the matter was decided on a purely financial basis.

LEAVELL'S PRINCIPLES FOR BAPTIST STUDENT UNION

Pioneering as the Baptist Young People's Union (BYPU) leader of Georgia since 1913, Frank Leavell was uniquely prepared for the tremendous new task he undertook. BYPU was the "doctrinal arm" of Southern Baptist churches. Through this organization young people learned what it meant to be a Baptist. Historical Baptists would point to the emphasis change of this organization in the late 1960s as one of the reasons for "the controversy" of fundamentalism—what Baptists believed was a natural part of their young people's religious growth.

Because of his tenure in Georgia, the new leader of college and university students realized the imperativeness for a denominational (translated, "conserve for Baptists") student program. He exclaimed years later, "We were losing at the top, losing all we had put into them through the years in BYPU. It had to be stopped."

Four Basic Principles

The four foundational principles for the Southwide Baptist student program (1) BSU was frankly denominational, (2) the emphasis was on student initiative, (3) the local church was supreme, and (4) students deserved the best program.[10]

The first principle was a narrow one. No pun was intended when Frank Leavell said the program was to be *frankly* denominational. Unfortunately, other denominations for seventy-five years have interpreted BSU in Leavell's manner. When authors of campus ministry books are chastised for not including the nation's—if not, the world's—largest campus ministry program in their writings, the answer always has been "your group has never participated on the ecumenical level."

That may have been true in the beginning; it is not true now nor has it been for three or more decades. Many local campus ministers' programs include ecumenical levels. It is also true that this same group understands ecumenicity is not to interfere or take the place of what their denomination has asked them to do. Nonetheless, during the first secretary's tenure, his first concern was to minister to the denomination's own. Leavell's words echoed, it was Baptist student work, without prejudice and without apology.

The second principle was unique. Leavell believed in students' ability to assume leadership. He was trying to do away with the old adage that college days were "only preparation for life." College days were life! Christian students, with all their potential, had an inescapable obligation to be prepared for Christian witness as they studied.

The third principle, one can safely assume—the supremacy of the local church—became the cardinal one. BSU did not function for itself alone. In this era a student did not belong to the organization until she or he was a member of a local church, or one of its unit organizations—Sunday School or BYPU. The only exceptions were membership in BSU's own unit groups—Young Women's Auxiliary, Young Men's Brotherhood, or Religious Volunteer Fellowships. Although the term today is a shibboleth, BSU was "the link between campus and church." Its whole program was planned to that end.

In perusing the memorial issue of the *Baptist Student*, dedicated to the first secretary of Southern Baptists' student program, one finds his primary motto, "Methods are many, principles few; methods often change, principles never do."

The local church principle, or conservation for a denomination, hardly changed from January 1, 1922, to Leavell's death December 7, 1949.

The fourth principle arose as a practical one and as a supplement to the second one—give the students the best! Cursory examinations of the programs at student weeks at Baptists' assemblies, Southwide Baptist student conferences, and youth conferences of the Baptist World Alliance (BWA), filled with renowned national and world personalities, prove that students received the best. Publications from the Southwide Student Department were outstanding. Even program personalities—paid mostly by the Southwide office—for state BSU conventions were leaders with regional and national reputations.

OTHER ASPECTS OF LEAVELL'S STUDENT PHILOSOPHY

To paint a complete picture of the first Southwide student secretary's philosophy, one needs to canvass other aspects of his thinking. It colored, in time, the concept of what Southern Baptists thought was BSU. These aspects were his view of interdenominationalism, his obsession with BSU work becoming international, and his concept of maximum Christianity.

Leavell's View of Interdenominationalism

Because of his strong denominationalism, Leavell often had to defend his idea of interdenominationalism. He admitted the appeal ecumenicity had for students—it was intriguing because of its broadness. He stated that Christian unity movements usually favor church union, disparage denominational distinction, and taboo doctrinal emphasis. He did admit that Baptist students were often embarrassed by his position. His illustration, strangely, was their embarrassment because of the lack of the suggested changes in regard to race by Baptists—especially the Negro [his term] race.

Parenthetically, this statement, and similar incidents in later years, would lead people to believe Leavell was not willing to attack such troubling issues of the 1940s. During that era, however, the racial discussions were only academic rhetoric. A native of Mississippi he was, but he could hardly be branded a racist. Yet, through these years at Ridgecrest meetings and other conferences, no African-American students and no African-American leaders were platform speakers.

Something happened during the tenure of Leavell to abdicate the program's beginning concerning African Americans. As early as the first All-Southern Baptist Student Conference at Birmingham, Alabama, in 1926, there were photographs of both Native and African Americans in the printed proceedings following the conference. The proceedings stated the following:

> . . . the race problem was not discussed extensively as though it was an immediate campus problem. The conference, however, did not fail to recognize the

issue. The representatives of all the different races were called to the front of the platform. . . . They sang together "Blest be the tie that binds our hearts in Christian love." Immediately the entire congregation arose and then the song was repeated in unison. That was one of the high points of the conference program and, accordingly, *it was voted as the answer of the conference to the race problem* [italics mine].[11]

Whether or not the rising tensions of race relations in later years quelled Leavell's work in this integrated beginning is a matter of conjecture.

Because of his relationship with Scott Edward Grinstead, an African American, one may think that Leavell was still thinking as a "separate but equal" person in the 1940s. Leavell employed Grinstead as consultant to students on blacks' campuses; he was always present at student weeks and other conferences. The "Prayer Calendar" of *Missions Mosaic* in June of 1996 reminded everyone what this man accomplished on black campuses during that era. Grinstead worked arduously; by 1967—long after Leavell's and his relationship began—fifty-six black Baptist Student Unions were active on college campuses in seventeen states.

In ecumenical endeavors, the Baptist student leader's participation was noted by H. D. Bollinger, secretary of the Board of Higher Education for the Methodist Church. He recalled, "Dr. Leavell always attended ecumenical staff meetings, made his reports, but did not participate in the deliberations." He added, "The greatest philosophical weakness of Southern Baptist student work is its lack of willingness to work with similar Christian groups. If Southern Baptists and Methodist students had worked together in the South all these years, what a difference it would have made!"[12] These remarks are charitable, yet candid, about a dear friend of many years.

This Baptist movement was a denominational one. Its approach was positive without being derogatory of other groups. Leavell, in the long run, found himself taking defensive measures to maintain this principle. He declared many times that people must learn to disagree agreeably.

An International Movement

The leader explored every possibility of making BSU an international movement, for his Christian heart was global in mission. The commission requested R. H. Rushbrook, program chair of BWA, to place an item on the BWA congress' agenda to present student work. This expansion of Southern Baptists' student program worldwide was considered in 1927.

Perhaps Leavell remembered how successful Mott had been with the World Student Christian Federation. He envisioned the same for Baptists. Soon after his request for one, the Youth Committee of BWA was formed with T. G. Dunning of England as chair and Leavell as secretary.

From the work of this committee emerged the first Baptist World Youth Congress in Prague, Czechoslovakia, during 1931. Only war has interrupted these meetings, which have been scheduled every five years since the initial one. The first youth secretary was Joel Sorenson of Sweden; he was followed by Robert S. Denny. Denny was a Southern Baptist student-work veteran who eventually became the general secretary of BWA.

FMB personnel recognized the validity of the secretary's dream. They sent him to the Far East and South America to "preach the gospel" of campus ministry. He may have acted as if the means and methods of Southern Baptists' BSU were the only viable ones, but Leavell recognized other methods for other countries.

As a result of this journey FMB had to reconsider its methods of conducting campus ministry—a reconsideration that took many years. During the 1940s and 1950s the individual mission group in each country determined the work of its missionaries. Campus ministry often was only part of the duties of a particular missionary. (There is a notation in the convention annual of 1944 that Edgar Hallock was sent by FMB to Brazil in 1942 to do student work.)

This policy caused almost no Baptist student secretaries to volunteer for foreign missions. Not being guaranteed their God-called vocation would be honored overseas, they did campus ministry at home. Winston Crawley, FMB's secretary to the Orient, announced at a 1959 BSU meeting in Nashville that all future appointments of personnel as student workers on foreign mission fields would be honored.

As the Baptist pioneer in student work had attacked problems at home, he also attacked those of the world. He had successfully executed his philosophy in SBC; he did the same with his ideas of a world denominational movement through BWA. Youth were the only hope that Christianity would not be extinct in the next generation. He was a Christian internationalist.

In paying tribute to this man, Dunning asserted the following:

> He was an internationalist able to comprehend and enrich all other loyalties. It did not suppress or impair a deep love for home and country. . . . Doctor Leavell's internationalism was practical. . . . While interested in the political and economic aspects of international problems, Dr. Leavell was sure they were but surface aspects of deep problems whose final solutions were spiritual.[13]

Maximum Christianity

A third aspect of Leavell's philosophy imbedded in his four basic BSU principles was his idea of maximum Christianity. This may have been the most controversial, yet it colored much of what BSU was and would become. Also, maximum Christianity determined the type of people attracted to the vocation of Baptist student secretary. This concept contributed to BSU's struggles in the late 1930s and through the 1940s in becoming a proven philosophy. Would this idea challenge the inhabitants of academe? Was Leavell's type of Christianity intellectually viable in this rarefied air?

From inception, denominational conservation was the cornerstone of Southern Baptists' student work. The program was a counteraction to what some thought, including Leavell, were subchristian standards on collegiate campuses. There is difficulty in proving this idea, but glances through Southwide programs of this time give some enlightenment. If subchristian standards on campuses existed, courage was required to declare them and to be true to the Christian position. Also, those who stood openly for the vital Christ would not be in the mainstream of campus life. Leavell contributed to this emphasis by his own concept of maximum Christianity.

The secular and religious press left the impression that Baptist students were different from their counterparts on the collegiate scene. The *Watchman Examiner*, the Northern Baptist publication, editorially headlined, "No Bolshevism Exists among Southern Students." The *Christian Index* of Georgia editorialized, "Southern Baptist Students Stand Firm on Fundamentals of Our Faith!" "The Problem of Personal Piety" received extensive press coverage of the first All-Southern Baptist Student Conference in Birmingham. A secular newspaper, the *Nashville Tennessean*, ran this headline on its front page during the 1925 Baptist Student Convention in that city: "Petting Parties, Immodesty, Unclean Living, Condemned at Students' Meet."[14]

Leavell's "worldliness out" ideas became the inspiration to launch the Master's Minority Movement. He was giving an address at the 1925 All-Student Conference when seemingly on a burst of unplanned inspiration came the exclamation, "You are a minority from your campus. You are the Master's Minority!" Four years later at a similar meeting, the Master's Minority Movement began. Leavell inaugurated it by saying:

> We pause to launch the Master's Minority Movement. The essence of it is to call out individuals to greater consecration, to greater usefulness. There is power in a determined minority; the power of the "saving few" has been the wonder of the ages. . . . The curse of Christendom is the ordinary Christian. I call you to the heights! But it will be a costly venture, and prayer will be the heart of it. Now we launch a movement. None of us know where it will lead. We launch it! Let God lead on.[15]

Participants said the audience was electrified, and the movement spread quickly. It buttressed the minority, members were unapologetic in their witness, and it was an evangelistic force among students across the South.

The Master's Minority brought changing programs on local campuses. However, the majority of students did not benefit because the minority members developed a "spiritual-elitist" attitude that did not endear them to other "BSUers." Leavell's concept was for more mature persons than novice adults. Those who led local work in the early 1940s began to take a jaundiced look at the movement. Leaders like Chester Durham, Kentucky's state student secretary; Robert Denny at

Baylor University; Howard Rees of Washington, D.C.; and Avery Lee of LSU had different ideas about the demise of the Master's Minority.[16]

Durham considered this phase of BSU its chief philosophical weakness. He asserted that the results of "calling out the few" to the student center across the street from academe precluded the possibility of penetrating the campus. Denny, soon to be a colleague in the Nashville office, observed that perhaps Master's Minority was a misunderstood term. Rees indicated that in the early 1940s a resistance developed to the strong pietistic emphasis of the movement. Lee concurs with Rees:

> Because of the Master's Minority Movement there developed an inner circle of students who felt superior to other students from a spiritual viewpoint. They had a "halo-complex." Even today the Baptist Student Union combats the problem of the inner circle and this may be because the adult leadership remembers the original concept of the Master's Minority.[17]

The movement faltered when efforts were made to organize it. The creative effectiveness was diminished. Organization became more important than spiritual intent. By 1949 the idea of Baptist Student Unions moving on the feet of its spiritual minorities had almost disappeared from student work.

In 1940 Leavell felt a need to defend his concept of maximum Christianity. He editorialized these interpretations: It did not mean sinless perfection; it did mean a holy discontent with one's spiritual achievement. Maximum Christianity is individual and not collective; some lives give Christ prominence, others preeminence. Low aim and not failure is sin; conquest is the price of spiritual growth.[18]

CONCLUSION

The first secretary—the one with the longest tenure (1922–1949)—had his critics about his principles and philosophy, especially the concept of maximum Christianity. Claude Broach, an early associate in the Nashville student department and the only biographer of Leavell, summarized this era:

> I used to feel that BSU was a movement which was under pressure to become an organization. Now I'm not so sure it was a movement—or that it could be called that today. It had tremendous impact in behalf of personal commitment and morality in the 30s—the days I knew it as a student. This began to be irrelevant to a world in the agony of World War II. The years since seem to me an effort to find a *raison d'être*.[19]

At this particular time, Broach was more than likely correct; however, the work did hammer out on the anvil of determination a reason to exist in future years.

Leavell's philosophy became the foundation for Southern Baptist campus ministry and it reflected the personality of the gentleman from Mississippi. His personal life was—still is—an immeasurable shadow over Baptists' campus ministry.

Birthing movements are almost always the reflection of the individual who inaugurated them. As with synonymy between YMCA and John R. Mott, BSU *was* Frank Hartwell Leavell Sr. for twenty-seven years. Yet, after a quarter of a century plus two years, only Baptists in academic situations understood the possibilities of BSU. The diamond was in a formative stage—fragile, uncut, unpolished, but struggling in the making. Decades would pass for it to become a sparkling missionary gem among Southern Baptists.

The Baptist Student Secretary
(Untrained but Dedicated)

Three developments from the 1930s to the end of the 1940s provided the foundation for the philosophy of Southern Baptists' student movement on college campuses. First, the vocation of the local Baptist student secretary arose; second, Frank Leavell provided materials to help this untrained but dedicated personnel; and third, both weaknesses and strengths of this infant movement surfaced.

THE VOCATION OF THE BAPTIST STUDENT SECRETARY

This vocation was not new, for YMCA and other religious organizations had also employed leaders in their work for many years. Defining leadership roles was an evolving process for Baptists. Local Baptist Student Unions organized before full-time personnel were available. Dedicated volunteer laypersons from the campus community or faculty from the academic one were the adult leaders for the first student religious groups.

Secretary Leavell viewed the spirituality of students as the most important aspect of their being. Therefore, he believed those who were to lead should be the most important and capable in the church community or on campus. In a speech before the Council of Church Boards of Education, Leavell coined a phrase that would epitomize the campus student secretary for years—the phrase "spiritual coach." He told the participants:

> On most campuses for men there will be found from one to four full-time athletic coaches. It is the responsibility of these . . . to discover the possibilities within the student body for teams. . . . There is need for athletic coaches. There is a greater need for spiritual coaches.[1]

The appellation "spiritual coach" served to identify Baptist student secretaries in the early years. Their quest was to find the maximum spiritual capacity for every student and to develop the student to that capacity.

The qualification for a local student secretary was set high. "Few other fields of religious work demand a more versatile and talented personality," Leavell said.[2] The minimum degree expected was a master of arts. This requirement is worthy of note because this may have been the first vocation among Southern Baptists in the 1930s to specify a certain educational background. More than likely, however, few met this ambitious criterion.

Spiritually, this vocational choice was one that required character beyond reproach. Leavell emphasized this need:

> Concerning qualifications those in the field have made the following sugges-tions: "Trained in order to demand the respect of both students and faculty;" "Should be an uncompromising Christian and a loyal Baptist;" "College b[r]ed with a keen desire for more education;" "Soul-winner; Resourceful; Missionary vision."[3]

The pioneer Leavell searched the South for the type of people he coveted for the student secretarial ranks. His persuasiveness, coaxing, challenging, and desire for the best caused people to feel flattered that he considered them worthy of the task.

Many factors, however, caused a turnover in the vocation. A great number of the early workers were women, primarily because of low salaries; many of them left when they married. Men often looked upon this position as a stepping-stone to a city pastorate (preferably a collegiate church), foregoing the time they other-wise may have had to prove themselves in a smaller, rural area. Also, World War II depleted leadership as many potential candidates went in large numbers to serve their country.

The biggest factor causing turnover, one that would follow the work like a shadow through the coming decades, was that the Baptist student program still had not been proclaimed sufficiently to the majority of Southern Baptists. The average Baptist could not see the need for additional expenditures of time, personnel, and money for campus work. At the same time, personnel at Baptist colleges looked upon this work as a threat to the mission of their own institutions. Thus, by the time of Leavell's death in 1949, the vocation had not become a profes-sion in the same sense as other church-related ones.

Leavell said these secretaries should be employed with the understanding that they are to rank on a parity with faculty members and paid not less than the average faculty salary.[4] In all his writings, this is the only mentioning of financial security of BSU secretaries. The opinion of most of his colleagues in student work was that this subject was not one of his primary concerns. If the Lord was leading a person into this vocation, Leavell felt little else mattered. His motto seems to have been "Lord, you keep them humble; we'll keep them poor."

Despite all of these factors contributing to excessive turnover, the standards set by Frank H. Leavell for leaders of college students were perhaps his greatest contribution to the development of a new church-related work. This position of campus student secretary would become a unique one in Southern Baptist life.

PUBLICATIONS FOR STUDENT MINISTRY

A variety of ambitious publications quickly became part of the foundation of giving students the best. The *Baptist Student* magazine debuted in September–October 1922. In his initial editorial, Leavell sought to involve the readers: "The columns of the *Baptist Student* will fail in their mission unless the students . . . make them the forum of their ideas and opinions, and for promoting their worthy plans."[5]

A quarter of a century later, the editor judged that the magazine had become a forum of student expression, a pictorial of campus life, a medium of good short stories, a review of life experiences of students, a help for religious leaders, a unifier of student religious effort, a stabilizer of students' faith, a touch of eminent educators, a confirmation of student convictions, and a clarion call to Christian service.[6]

The periodical for its first three and one-half decades shows that the ambitious goals were fulfilled. By the 1960s the magazine had become more intellectual in content than it was in the early days, a change reflecting different student concerns. Later issues grappled with subjects such as race, war, and the changing roles of women in the nation and church. A major weakness of the early publication was the first editor's apparent deliberate omission of social issues. The possibility of controversy had no place in Leavell's spiritual ideology.

Once the *Baptist Student* was established, the first book on methods of organization was published in 1927. The *Baptist Student Union Methods* soon became the official manual for student leaders. Revisions occurred twice—in 1935 and 1944—but little was changed from the original. Principles were given practical interpretation by the methods outlined for effective work in the local, state, national, and international scene.

The principles found expression through organization and planning. Claude Broach, Leavell's colleague at the time, observed the following:

> B. S. U. was more than an organization. It was a spiritual movement under-girded by a dynamic power. Frank had proved [by his methods book] that he knew how to build an organization without losing sight of the spiritual purposes for which the organization must ever be only a means to an end.[7]

Whether or not the organizational manual produced a movement is an aside. At least a method was found to introduce Leavell's principles broadly and give to them practical expression. Little changed in this foundation volume until 1957. David Alexander and G. Kearnie Keegan's volume, the *Baptist Student Union Manual*, redefined the expanding program of BSU.

A third group of publications worthy of note was the My Covenant series, starting in 1940, which came out of the Master's Minority Movement of 1925 and the covenant that accompanied it. Each section of the covenant became the title of a separate book written by different people, each expressing and expanding upon Leavell's ideals. The titles were *Salvation, Worldliness Out, Bible Study, Prayer and Meditation, Church Loyalty, Sabbath Observance, Christian Ownership,* and *Christian Witnessing.*

The Hazen Books on Religion were published by the Hazen Foundation, an ecumenical religious group, just three years prior to the My Covenant series. Possibly Leavell conceived of these books from the earlier publications. He "borrowed" freely from others. One example was the development of religious focus weeks in Baptist schools, according to Broach:

> In January of 1939 Frank was invited by Dr. Jesse M. Bader to participate in a "University Christian Mission" on the campus of the University of Georgia. Responding to the invitation, he saw in this new approach to campus religious life—something which held great promise if it could be adapted to denominational schools.[8]

Despite his guarded views on interdenominationalism, this great denominationalist did not hesitate to use ideas from the Federal Council of Churches, which he otherwise ignored. If an idea was good and if it promised to benefit his students, he would take any idea from anywhere and adapt it. Therefore, when the Hazen books were published, surely he saw possibilities for the My Covenant series.

The covenant series became study guides and inspirational reading for students in the early 1940s. Leavell saw in these materials the possibility of furthering the Master's Minority Movement. However, the "elitist spirituality" brought about by this movement was waning, and newer student secretaries felt the elitism of the few was a detriment to the many. Soon after G. Kearnie Keegan arrived as the new Conventionwide (formerly known as Southwide) secretary in 1950, he noticed lessening sales of this series; by the early 1950s, its publication ceased.

Of the many pamphlets and other materials published, a final one merits discussion: *A Standard of Requirements: First Magnitude.* This publication was offered for Baptist Student Unions as "other standards of requirements" or "standards of excellence" had been for church organizations. Both phrases were used interchangeably for Baptist Sunday Schools and doctrinal training groups. The general headings for *First Magnitude* were Organization and Procedure, Enlistment Program, Christian Witnessing and Practical Service, Denominational Meetings and Movements, and Christian Culture.[9]

First Magnitude was an effort to evaluate the success of each organization (and for "bragging rights" over the convention). Doyle J. Baird, a Sunday School Board Student Department consultant, judged it less than fully effective:

For many years the *First Magnitude—Standard of Requirements* has been posed as a tool in evaluating the program of Baptist Student Unions. Its chief value is in its attempt to evaluate as to balance of meetings, activities, organization, and emphases. [He added, however] Numbers of Baptist Student directors have expressed doubts as to its reliability as an evaluating device and have expressed a discontent with it.[10]

The difficulty in measuring results in Christian education cannot be denied, but growth on the part of students involved in a program during their collegiate careers should have some basis for evaluation. Perhaps assessment of students' Christian attitudes, ethical discrimination, and spiritual depth would give a better measurement than measuring facets of the organization itself. Leavell's attempt at devising *First Magnitude* requirements at least led to studying other methodologies, whereby the development of Christian attitudes and, thus, the successes of BSU work could be determined.

The rise of the vocation of what Leavell called the "Baptist Student Religious Secretary" on each campus and the publications of the national student department added much to the promotion of the philosophy of BSU as seen by Frank Leavell. The vocation has changed, so have the publications; however, Leavell's efforts gave students a superior foundation for the work and the worker.

THE WEAKNESSES AND STRENGTHS OF
EARLY BAPTIST STUDENT UNIONS

The significance of the first twenty-seven years of Southern Baptist student work under Leavell cannot ever be fully articulated. The fundamental philosophy as developed by the first national secretary proved to be a sound foundation. Tom J. Logue, former state student director of Arkansas, once observed, "The concept of the early B.S.U. as a link between college and church was almost landmark emphasis."[11]

Building a movement with an intense denominational concern, BSU experienced phenomenal growth in early years. Although Southern Baptists as a whole were not immediately cognizant of the efforts of the movement, its acceptance among students far exceeded the fondest dreams of even those most closely connected to the work. However, as in the majority of young movements, both weaknesses and strengths became apparent.

Weaknesses of Early Baptist Student Unions
Generally, four weaknesses were apparent:
1. The lack of trained leadership was evident because this vocation was too often regarded as a secondary, or transitional, calling.

2. BSU did not speak to the student who had a weak church relationship or none.
3. The program lacked intellectual and social concern.
4. Southern Baptists, as a whole, were uninformed about the program and the successes of this early campus movement. This remains a modern-day problem.

The major weakness was the lack of trained campus secretaries. Lay leaders, untrained in biblical and theological knowledge, were called upon to launch this new church-related vocation.

Leavell thought a masculine image was imperative, but men did not linger long before moving to a pastorate. The national leader would say to colleagues, "Don't put skirts on our work. You will never have real strong men to follow feminine leadership" (this was the 1940s). Whether or not Dr. Frank's paranoia was valid may not be important. However, for these reasons, early Baptist laborers in the vineyards of higher education became popularizers of the faith rather than professional soldiers on the battleground of ideas in academe.

Because of the prevalence of transient, untrained leadership—dedicated pioneers though they were—BSU degenerated in the late 1930s and early 1940s to a social and recreational emphasis. This shift of activity almost provided its death knell. (One informal characterization personified the position of BSU secretary as requiring an "Alka Seltzer personality" who wore sport coats, bow ties, and argyle socks; played the piano; and was able to make and serve Kool Aid and cookies. Because of the "alka seltzerness," secretaries often fizzed out after approximately eighteen months and sought other employment.)

A second major weakness, thought by some student leaders of this period, was almost a contradiction of what most viewed its primary strength—church conservation. If one analyzes the total program, there is validity to their concern. Howard Rees, a veteran even during this period, maintained, "One of the major weaknesses of the movement is found in that it did not speak to the student who did not come from a strong church relationship. The Baptist Student Center became a ghetto for religious students who did not have a concern for the life of the total campus."[12]

The "ghetto" problem would not go away even as the program became more sophisticated through the decades. Baptist students, like the Jews who saw Jerusalem as the place where God dwelt, too often have thought the Baptist student center is their Jerusalem.

A third weakness was the initial lack of intellectual and social concern. This was particularly evident in Baptists' lack of interest in what other student denominational groups were doing concerning theological and social issues. "BSUers" thought they alone enjoyed their ride to heaven. Roman Catholics with their Newman Clubs and the Jewish with their B'nai B'rith Hillel Foundations were not riding in the high-occupancy vehicle lanes bound for the promised land. Protestant groups—the Methodists' Wesley Foundations and Presbyterians' Westminster

Fellowships—were only challengers for everyone to get involved ecumenically on an intellectual and social action level. According to Rees, "B. S. U. was isolated from the other streams on the campus so that it did not contribute to the total impact of the Christian faith on campus."[13] He was correct. (A note: The omission of vertical—humankind to God—issues by Protestant campus groups, who banded as interdenominationalists in the 1960s, almost caused their demise.)

A final weakness is one that is still prevalent. Southern Baptists during Leavell's tenure chose to remain uninformed as to the philosophy, work, and programs of their denominational campus movement. A dichotomy existed between Baptist student work and denominational education. Because of the largely rural and uneducated background of Southern Baptist people of the era, the whole scope of education was suspect. In their view academe and church were—and are— perilous partners. The hope of every generation of student workers since 1922 has been that this problem of communication will be solved as the general constituency becomes more educated. Unfortunately, many in the pew are ahead of those behind the sacred desk in recognizing the corollary between the intellectualism of Athens and the spirituality of Jerusalem.

Strengths of Early Baptist Student Unions

The progress of the work was rapid. Through the years BSU proved adaptable to any academic community; it linked multitudes to the church; its evangelistic emphasis led nonchristians to the Savior; it influenced scores of young people to become "maximum" Christians, and all this was accomplished without weakening any existing church organizations.

The remarkably rapid growth of BSU in the first decade proved that denominational student movements had great potential. The evidence of progress is shown in Leavell's 1927 report—written only five years after he assumed leadership: "From the first we have thought in terms of a five year period. . . . Looking at it from the viewpoint of tangible results, we have realized more than we actually and reasonably expected."[14]

The second strength was the international emphasis that Leavell, primarily, envisioned for the program. World emphasis in student work in the formative years can be directly attributed to BSU's early work in this field.

A third strength, little recognized, was the emphasis upon each student becoming a mature Christian. For Baptist students the emphasis was living the lordship of Christ according to their own capacity. This brought maturation—adolescent though it might have been. There were times when the program was guilty of pointing to the church-related volunteer, the scholar, the beauty queen, or the athlete as examples of what the organization had accomplished. On the whole, though, the program encouraged all students to find unique paths to being like Christ.

This strength has set apart Baptist campus ministry from solitary evangelical programs such as Campus Crusade for Christ and InterVarsity. Many students appear at Baptist student centers, seeking a campus minister after having had an initial experience with God through Christ amid these nondenominational organizations. "Can someone teach me how to mature as a Christian? Can the program of BSU do that?" The answer has always been a resounding *yes!*

The greatest strength of this movement, and perhaps its cardinal principle, is its connection to the local church. The linked idea of student-campus-church has prevailed during these initial years and, in diverse ways, through three-fourths of the twentieth century. Above all, it has conserved Baptist students for its denomination. The church added its strength to protect students from what some consider subchristian standards prevalent on secular campuses around the South.

W. F. Howard, state student director of Texas during the expansion period of BSU work, observed on the fiftieth anniversary of this movement that its strengths and weaknesses are almost the same as those in Leavell's tenure. BSU, Howard noted, has been strong because it tried to be a valid part of higher education and yet not lose the uniqueness of its mission. Second, BSU was strong because it had been inclusive and not exclusive. He meant that the movement had tried to present the whole gospel for the whole person. Third, the Texan did not apologize for structure and organization in order to accomplish the purposes of Baptist student ministries. Rightly, he points to other campus ministries that eschewed structures as undesirable in student movements. Last, BSU has been strong because it has remembered its heritage as a supporting movement of church and denomination.[15]

Howard, a realist, acknowledged that all movements do have weaknesses. He pointed to at least five in Baptist campus ministry. The Texas director said BSU has been weak to the extent its purposes have not been fully understood by the larger group of Southern Baptists. The first weakness may not have been as much BSU's fault as that of the church and denomination. Second, BSU has allowed itself to become shackled by the same cultural patterns that frequently plague churches. This was a just and severe criticism when freedom of ideas is the hallmark of academia. Third, Howard pointed to the "either-or" dilemma, the endless and exasperating debates on what to emphasize: evangelism or ministry, churchmanship or social action. Broad concepts of BSU purposes resolve this dilemma. Fourth, BSU has been weakened when professional leadership becomes preoccupied with the search for meaningful personal roles. This was true, particularly at the time Howard wrote. One role that obscured all others was the adopted *new* one of counselor—whether or not leadership had been trained in this field. Last, BSU is weakened when leadership is no longer interested in the "essential basics" to which the denomination had been committed for a half-century: Bible study, prayer, God's will for students' lives, churchmanship, world missions, and learning to share personal faith in Jesus Christ.[16] Perhaps the leadership in the 1990s should think more on the essential basics. When strengths and weaknesses are measured against each other, the strengths easily outweigh the weaknesses. The success of Leavell's years were followed by a period of tremendous growth.

THE END OF AN ERA

Frank Leavell died of a worn-out heart on December 7, 1949, and was buried in Oxford, Mississippi, among the other famous Leavell legends of Southern Baptist history. (If one could have looked into that heart, surely they would have seen the initials *BSU* carved across the broadest part.) In its stead, he left another heart for Southern Baptists in the student program that was his creation. Its rhythms beat in young maturing Christian students who are their denomination's missionaries at home and abroad.

Let no one forget that those who create Christian homes, provide leadership in local churches, who pray for and finance others called in full-time Christian service, are themselves "on mission." Dr. Frank's death was the end of an era for the Baptist Student Union. His legacy is great.

An Expanding Movement
(The Solidifying of a Vocation)

The BSU insignia, a three-linked chain with the words Campus-Student-Church inside, served well as a reminder of a denomination's conservation of students for three decades. The Leavell years produced a dynamic and successful program that developed because of its philosophy. In many ways, the type of student—a dedicated Christian with high moral values—made the work easy. The typical student had overcome the Great Depression, World War II, and the Korean conflict. Each of these crises had a tendency to drive students toward the Christian faith.

The campus ministers of the 1950s made their reputation on students who were easily enlisted in BSU. In the words of the baseball movie, *Field of Dreams,* "Build it and they will come." The adult leaders opened the student centers in the South, and the students came!

However, changes followed World War II. Increased higher-education enroll-ment brought diversified students—no longer only single ones, eighteen to twenty-two years of age. The homogeneity of the campus was shattered and educational segmentation began. As educational campus life was historically changed, so would future programs of religious organizations respond. A philo-sophical *raison d'être* for Baptist Student Unions needed to be determined instead of simple activities of devotion and denominational conservation.

Baptist student secretaries became directors of Baptist student ministries. Since the 1950s this title evolved, and in 1970 state student directors finally adopted it officially. The term "secretary" was too confusing for those in the academic world. Questions like "Whose secretary are you?" did not give much, if any, accreditation.

This period was also the beginning of Baptist agencies, state and national, adopting business-management principles for spiritual purposes. These principles were thought to help enlist more people in churches and more finances for Baptist state conventions and agencies. Later, management groups were employed such as Booze, Allen and Hamilton (derisively referred to during coffee breaks as the "Trinity"—notice the absence of the word *Holy*). Their management principles did cause churches to become more successful. Who can forget slogans like "A Million More in '54?" Agency money did increase because of the suggestions of these fore-runners of today's management ideas. However, they may have had numerous effects on the "spirituality" of Baptists in that day and this.

Changing factors indicated that expanding programs would have to take root not only on local campuses but also in the various state student departments if student work was to continue to grow and remain viable for a new campus constituency. Single, undergraduate students in four-year curriculum universities were still the major focus of Baptist campus ministry. These students lived in dormitories or in the collegiate community. The only new innovation was summer missions.

Campus ministers' dilemmas rose with the realization that increasing numbers of students were unlike the traditional student of the past. Metropolitan and commuting schools, along with graduate students, were becoming numerous. Married students were now a permanent part of campus life. Numerous international students came to learn technological skills that this nation abundantly possessed. Some leaders advocated that BSU had a responsibility to faculty.

The Christian faith is valid for each of these groups. Because each possessed their own peculiar needs, new programs had to be developed. Not only were students diverse; so were the institutions involved. Richard Ostheimer observed, "Diversity is so great in fact, that if one attempts to get perfectly homogenous classifications, one approaches the absurdity of finding that the number of classifications equal[s] the number of institutions to be classified."[1]

G. Kearnie Keegan became Frank Leavell's successor May 1, 1950. He was a man of many talents. In prior years Keegan had been a pastor, a local church religious-education director, and was the first state student director in Louisiana. He was a musician, and those who knew him still recall the image of him sitting at the piano playing and singing in baritone voice "Old Man River" and his signature hymn, "The Lily of the Valley."

During his tenure as the second Conventionwide student secretary, which ended with his death September 13, 1960, Keegan realized that changes in BSU programming were imperative if a new student constituency was going to be reached for God and church. Whether or not he knew how to accomplish this task will forever be a moot question. However, at the time, no one knew how. At the least he was not afraid to try, but it was not until December 1962 that a stated unified philosophy and objectives for Southern Baptist student work was accomplished.

In the middle twentieth century both campuses and the world were fragmenting. The widespread notion that during the 1950s "the bland was leading the bland" proved fallacious. This decade incubated the turbulent 1960s. The Christian faith, if it was to permeate the "halls of ivy," was being called upon to provide leadership for whole people in a fragmented world. In a book published in 1964, Verlyn Barker, then secretary for Campus Ministry for the United Church of Christ, emphasized, "The day of the recreational leader and popularizer of the faith has gone forever; the day has arrived when the church must raise up men [and women] who can participate in the battle of ideas."[2] He could have just as rightly written this the previous decade.

A student may be an undergraduate, married international. Into which category should she/he be placed? Problems like this faced student leadership. Categories cannot be exhaustive or exclusive. The ultimate truth in campus ministry is that each student needs ministering according to his or her spiritual needs at specific times.

CHARACTERIZING DIFFERENT TYPES OF STUDENTS

Local campus ministers needed to program for different types of students; at the time they knew only how to program for the single undergraduate. Realizing that, early in 1958, Keegan appointed "commissions" to study the needs of those who did not fit the historical successful program. The purpose of the commissions was to study new ways of "doing" evangelism, missions, and Christian maturation. He hoped, in the end, to create a uniform philosophy of student work for Southern Baptists.

Community Colleges

The growth of junior, now called community, and metropolitan colleges was evident as students found themselves at college age but with little finances to "go to the big university." They were adolescents who were not mature enough to be comfortable away from home. More students who were at "the big university" drove there each day from home. George W. Jones, then BSU director at Vanderbilt University, was chairman of the commuter commission. This group defined a commuter as "any student who does not live in a dormitory or other near-campus housing." In a report of seventy-five BSU directors in 1959, it was noted that 57 percent of students to whom they ministered were commuters. At the same time, those directors who worked in community colleges reported their ministry consisted of 93 percent commuters.[3]

Nell Magee, who was a consultant concerning community colleges in the Sunday School Board office, prophesied the following:

> In this decade [1960s] . . ., five hundred new colleges are to be established . . ., and most of them will be public[ly] supported community colleges with little or no dormitory facilities. They will draw students from surrounding areas who can commute daily. It is increasingly important that *most* of our churches have a ministry to students.[4]

This meant new duties for the BSU director. She/he needed to teach surrounding lay leaders and pastors how to relate to this novice adult who was also a college student, though still living at home. Magee was correct. This type of ministry was becoming more relevant.

Metropolitan Colleges

The metropolitan college was the new phenomena of the late 1950s. This type of university was generally characterized as a "concrete college." Georgia State University in downtown Atlanta is a prime example. The leaders of this new type of higher education were grasping for definite ideas about themselves and their students. Ideas were still fermenting in describing these constituents and in developing a philosophy for metropolitan education. Religious leaders were swimming in the many differences of those in city schools and found themselves trying ideas they had not been trained to accomplish. In many ways these students were far more in need of spiritual help than the normal collegians of the past.

James M. Hester, then president of New York University, was a strong advocate of metropolitan education. When asked why anyone would want to go to a college in the big city, especially one with no campus living, he mused in reply:

> Because many of today's young people want to be where the action is. We have become a city-oriented society. Going to college in the city gives a student the chance to see reality first hand, close-up. He doesn't have to live in a textbook world. Equally important are the city's tremendous diversity and intellectual and cultural vitality.[5]

The positive aspects of Hester's philosophy certainly bears consideration. However, several factors tend to give special characteristics to students involved in metropolitan education. Some are positive, but others have negative implications. Campus ministers to these students of the asphalt campus should be able to recognize them and plan accordingly to their needs.

Students living at home are daily under a variety of strains in the process of achieving independence from family. These strains affect study habits, motivations for study, and emphasis on grades. Strain also affects occupational objectives; religious, racial, and class prejudices; dating; and responses to peer pressure. Metropolitan universities tend to have absentee faculties, which means no symbolic characters give resident universities their image as academic communities. Finally, metropolitan universities tend to take on the character of the cities where they domicile—unusual proportions of religious, ethnic, or social groupings.

These general considerations, plus others, should not necessarily be considered liabilities. Urban universities have led to a new philosophy of education. The sheer determination it takes to get a metropolitan education creates an unusual earnestness in these students. Older students make mature leadership possible and give to campus life an implicit assumption that this is real life. Here was a new kind of student. The denomination had much to learn in devising a program to meet the needs of this type of academician.

Married Students

Robert Sanks, director of the Wesley Foundation at the University of Wisconsin, observed during the 1950s:

> We are concerned with a relatively new phenomenon. . . . Before World War II a married man was not only a rarity on the campus, but [he] was not in the best favor with college and university officials. Since 1945 this particular student has become a permanent part of the student body. On some campuses their classification is responsible for some 20 to 25% of the student body.[6]

Not until the enactment of the Government Issue (GI) bill did the sharp rise in married collegians occur. Other reasons were obvious in considering marriage. Four or five wartime years had passed; the soldier returned to civilian life, but found himself in new situations—not the least being more discomfort in living with parents. The girl he left to "save the nation for democracy" probably had finished her degree and was willing to earn her share of the family income. Above all reasons, the strong pull of affection security—the desire for home and companionship—was there. For the most part, the returning veteran's school record was good. The reason was that the spouses were determined to make the most of each educational opportunity. For many, if it had not been for the GI bill, higher education would have been an impossible dream.

The characteristics of married students helped to convey to campus religious leaders how to minister to them. Their primary characteristic was being a student. They may have been an undergraduate, graduate, or an international, but a student nonetheless. As Sanks observed, the church in its ministry had first to consider that quality:

> The church must call the married student to his real vocation within the academic community. It is easy to classify this student in other categories because of his family relationships. Many times he gives the impression of denying this role about being a student. There seems to be something immature about being a student in his way of thinking. The real tragedy of the married student often lies at this point of his confused role in life—that of being a student, and that of being married.[7]

Being a marriage partner was the second characteristic of this student. Spouses had and have a responsibility to and for each other. They often were parents. The wife was the one with complexities. She may have been the breadwinner, a homemaker, a mother, a student, and a marriage partner.

The wife and husband are also part of the university community. Cocurricular activities are as important to a complete education as being in the classroom. Educational experiences that lie beyond the campus make all students culturally and socially mature. Married folk should not be an exception. The rich life of the campus is there for the taking. Free music, recitals and lectures, intramural and collegiate athletics are abundant. Unfortunately, married students participate little, thus robbing themselves of a vital part of education.

The last characteristic of married collegians was that they may be exploited in the community, falling prey to landlords who generally charge more for apartments because of their proximity to campus. Consequently, married youngsters often have lived at a distance or in relics of the past. "Vetvilles" became the slums of the campus community.

The Commission on Married Students, chaired by S. L. Harris, a local campus minister in Texas, reported to the Expansion Commission,[8] the overall group charged with the task of developing a unified philosophy that Southern Baptists would have to take cognizance of this group's work if the good news was for all of God's campus creatures.

The Graduate and Medical Student

Although James O. Cansler, in 1966, chaired the Commission on Graduate Students, Howard Bramlette, who was consultant for graduate and professional schools in the Sunday School Board Student Department, made his contribution to this commission:

> Three fourths of all college seniors now say they plan to attend graduate school. . . . Not all of them are completely satisfied with the situation encompassing graduate study today, . . . the length of the doctoral program, the too-rigid curriculum, too formal teaching methods, "vested interests," and "dead traditions." Certainly, not all graduate students have the same religious orientation and background of faith. But they do have some things in common: ability, achievement, promise, purpose, perseverance.[9]

Bramlette was on target! In the late 1950s some educational institutions thought about becoming completely graduate ones. Two of those were Georgia Technological University and Tulane University. That did not happen, but religious leaders realized that more attention was going to be demanded concerning this group simply because of increased numbers. Also, graduate students had unique traits that needed analyzing for program purposes.

The first trait graduate students possess is they have peculiar emotional needs. Poor interpersonal relationships may be a primary reason they are in graduate schools. Also, many go into graduate work because of no definite vocational and few social goals. Emotional problems are made even more difficult by this student being singled out for special work and attention. The emotional stress of obtaining graduate degrees is obvious without involving persons with feelings of inadequacy.

Secondly, graduate students are faced with a lack of time. Time is a commodity to be rationed. Any religious program must take rationed time into consideration.

Organizational emphasis has to be sacrificed; programs must be qualitative, not quantitative. Especially for graduate students, every BSU and church must always ask the question whether or not plans are worth their time. If churches and campus religious organizations provide for the graduate student's need for intellectual vitality, causing him or her to recognize the relation of his or her vocation to the Christian faith, then the student's time will be properly utilized.

Parenthetically, the name for these groups in many instances are being changed. Graduate and medical students may feel they have had their "BSU experience" and are ready for something different. The names Baptist Medical Fellowship and Christian Graduate Group are serving well in this situation.

The conclusion of the Commission on Graduate Students about these students' need for intellectual vitality points the way for effective programming:

> If they are sufficiently concerned with the intellectual pursuit to be graduate students, they are concerned with objective truth. Therefore,
>
> 1. Only the highest caliber of program personnel can hope to be effective in confronting graduate students with the truths of the Gospel.
> 2. Only an intellectual and respectable presentation of the Gospel can claim attention.
> 3. Only the most relevant topics for discussion can move them to participation.
> 4. In an all too personal commitment, only the most intellectually valid and spiritually authentic invitation can move them to dedication.
> 5. In summation, the level of programs for graduate students must be very high in intellectual content and spiritual vitality.[10]

The last trait of the graduate student is the need to relate his or her faith to vocation. The Christian faith has needed to be seen as a perspective from which to view all of life. The task of graduate programs was and is to make the relationship of faith to the various disciplines obvious, intellectually attractive, and emotionally demanding. Medical students have had graduate students' needs and also some peculiar to their own vocation. Berkely L. Poole, during the late 1950s, was director of the Wesley Foundation at the University of Tennessee Medical Units. He defined the average medical student as follows:

> If I may use the curve of normal distribution, to the right is a minority grouping of fundamental conservatives, to nominally interested, to maturely concerned students; to the left is a small grouping of humanistic, to agnostic, to atheistic oriented students. The "average" medical student will be church members who see the church as "a good thing" and religion as "all right" with neither as a live option. The "average" medical student will tend not to go to church. He stays away not out of sophomoric rebellion but because "it doesn't offer me anything."[11]

Medical students can be understood, like other students, from the context of their home background. The great majority come from small town and country churches where fundamental theology may have been the source of their religious training. Because of geographical locations, these students probably have had a minimal exposure to the arts, music, and in-depth biblical interpretation. Their whole collegiate experience may have emphasized the natural sciences. That does color one's view concerning life in general, and emphasis on the supernatural in particular. The ministry to these students is to help bring about the leap of faith wherein effort will be made to fit the whole self into God's scheme of things.

This is a difficult task. Medical students, generally speaking, see mostly charity patients and life's seamier side. Administrative, faculty, and student relationships are acute in medical complexes because students are submissive to this hierarchy. This task is doubly difficult when the student is married. Marital problems are more frequent for two reasons: the lack of time for the development of relationships and the educational chasm that develops between spouses. While one is learning, the other—often the wife—is forced into the job market for the benefit of both. The job market is mostly demeaning in view of the spouse's previous collegiate education.

This era of campus ministry began to expand Baptist programs to include graduate and medical personnel. The question emerged whether campus ministers of the 1950s had been trained to challenge this scientific, intellectual group.

The International Student

International students, as a category, are difficult to classify. In addition to all of the individual differences that give American students a variety of personal differences, internationals are different in at least four cases: (1) The national status that the students feel is accorded their country, (2) the relevance of their present opportunities to their life expectations in a different culture, (3) the cultural distance between their own and this country, and (4) their familiarity with the English language.[12]

Students from around the globe may defy categorizing, yet some questions about them can be asked. Who are they? What are they like? What do they seek in this country? What is their attitude toward the Christian church in America?

From a Christian perspective, these students are fellow humans and creatures of God. Most of them are among the top echelon of their countries. They will return to assume leadership roles in government, industry, business, and education. Their years here—whether good or bad—could be determining factors in international relations and world peace. The international student is one facet of a many-sided composite, the international person who is the moving shuttle that weaves the fabric of any coming world civilization.

If campus ministers and American students are fortunate, they can make winning witnesses to these unusual folk across the nation, who could, in turn, share their spiritual experiences on returning home. This sharing could be in places and strata the foreign missionary would never be able to touch because of culture and language.

Students from other lands are here primarily to seek an education. Happiness, pleasure, and friendships are paramountly found with those of their own culture. These ethnic groups give them identity in a strange land. The materialism of America often puzzles them. Internationals cope by retreating to the comfort of others like themselves or, unfortunately, join Americans in the materialism of this nation.

Those who cope by retreating suspect the American religious scene is a part of the materialism. Few internationals give the Christian church their endorsement. They are aware of the failures of the church. They test the faith of Christians with their best ideals and standards. This is not only present-day thinking. Long ago Reginald Wheeler contended in a book for YMCA:

> Some church criticisms frequently pointed to are: sectarianism; discrepancies between the profession and practice of Christians; over socializing of churches, with the consequent loss of spiritual vitality; commercialization of management and methods; . . . dogmatic teachings; frivolity and moral and religious irresponsibility of [the] young people of the church.[13]

After nearly seventy-five years little has changed about Wheeler's comments as far as internationals are concerned. However, over the past two decades, campus ministry has reaped benefits from global missions because more Christian internationals have begun appearing—especially from Southeast Asia and a few from Africa. Some internationals from Africa changed Southern Baptist churches and Baptist campuses. (See Will Campbell's *The Stem of Jesse* about Mercer University and Baptist churches in Macon, Georgia, for an example.)

The Commission on Internationals reminded campus ministers of the importance of this group. A commission report articulated the needs of this group and specified programs for them. Among these were English classes along with Bible study groups for both Christian and nonchristian foreign students. BSU and church groups' social occasions became an opportunity for internationals to bring their country's favorite dishes.   State and regional Baptist groups began having international student retreats at Thanksgiving and Easter. American host families provided homes during longer holidays such as Christmas. This helped with students' loneliness, and the Advent season gave easy access to conversation about the baby Jesus who was the Christ of the ages. Church people helped by widening an old program—Church: Adopt an International!

TWO GROUPS REQUIRE MORE THAN CHARACTERIZATION

Two commissions during this 1958 study found themselves involved in more than characterization. One was advocating ministry to faculty. This work was questionable because it was not technically "student work." The other commission was charged with finding better ways to develop Baptist Student Unions on Southern Baptist college campuses, which again raised the question that had haunted those involved in campus ministry since 1924. What was the difference in Baptist Christian education and a missionary endeavor called Baptist Student Union?

Baptist Faculty

Some opposed this potential change in student work philosophy of advocating ministry to faculty. However, it was true that faculty needed to realize they were witnesses in academe. Not only should their vocation have had Christian overtones, but some in their group needed ministering. They didn't need to park Christ outside the classroom.

Two questions faced this commission: Is it the task of a campus student organization to minister to transitory people and the church to permanent residents? Could an organization that historically had dedicated itself to the Christian maturation of students communicate these ideas to adults?

Some positive criteria for this segment of campus life had to be faced. Howard Bramlette contended for extenuating considerations that must be given this group:

> The worth of a faculty member as a person. He is in need of redemption and Christian nurture. He is an exceptional person by reason of background, insight, and training. This is especially true because his vocational pursuit is primarily in the area of the mind.

> The member's relationship to students. Because he bears a significant leadership relationship as a catalyst, mediator, and source of inspiration, he is one of the most strategic persons in the students' search for truth and reality.[14]

Another consideration is the faculty member's relationship to the university. In the academy's effort to find truth, the Christian perspective is essential to the realization of the highest purposes of education. Faculty members are on the growing edge of knowledge. Because it is their vocation in the finest sense to hold knowledge, faculty members synergically exert influence in many areas of life out of proportion to their number.

Changes in education, particularly in state education and the declining influence of Christian colleges, found the church on the perimeter of higher education. As William B. Rogers, then the executive secretary of the Faculty Christian Fellowship of the National Council of Churches, maintained: "*The church is on the outside looking in.* Although there was a time in American history when the Protestant church largely dominated the educational process, especially at the college level, that day has long since passed."[15]

Bramlette did not write as strongly as Rogers, but he did recognize the tension between university and church. He saw the solution in a coalition between Baptist Faculty Fellowships and churches:

> The university challenges traditional views whereas the church often dismisses . . . any view that opposes tradition. Consequently, the faculty member is in need of reassurance which may be his in the warmth of Christian fellowship and must be recognized for the potential Christian witness he is. The churches are indispensable to the maturing spiritual, moral, and intellectual life of the faculty member. As the BSU represents a unified ministry to all the churches, . . . the Baptist Faculty Fellowship provides specialized activities on campus for faculty members.[16]

The problems of ministering to faculty were the same as those with graduate students. The lack of a clear self-image of BSU was detrimental. Traditionally, it had served the undergraduate; it had been viewed as a group that gathered for inspiration. Therefore, as suggested by James Cansler, "The work of campus ministry has been looked upon as recreation by some, missionary by most, and Christian higher education by few, if any."[17]

The Baptist student movement in efforts to include faculty members in the late 1950s depended on them for leadership more than on the campus minister. In many cases BSU leadership felt a new program was being forced upon them, and they probably felt incapable—they were not ready to minister to this adult constituency on the campus.

However, the commission felt that those in the Conventionwide Student Department should go ahead and devise a program for faculty. For a decade following, Howard Bramlette and Arthur Driscoll, leadership consultants in the Sunday School Board office, led this work. One of the most successful ideas was developing weekend regional conferences for faculty, staff, and other adminis-trators, where they heard well-known speakers who were Christians and also shared ideas with colleagues in academia.

By the 1970s this part of campus ministry from the Nashville central office became less necessary, primarily because local campus ministers—now more trained—were developing their own faculty programs. One example occurred at Northeast Louisiana University (NLU), where faculty requested programs more theological in nature and ecumenical in attendance. These programs filled a void the faculty recognized in their churches and demonstrated what Bramlette said in 1958. The NLU group, begun in 1973, has continued into 1997 as a "brown-bag" meeting, called the Theological Roundtable, congregating every two weeks.

Students in Baptist Higher Education

Baptist college students were supposed to be different from all others because of their environment. They have not been. Recapping, early in 1924 the first encounter between BSU and Baptist school philosophy began. Leavell insisted—and never wavered—that the Southern Baptist Education Board, an agency for Baptist schools, was founded on the basis of Baptist academic and curriculum development. BSU, Leavell insisted, was founded as a missionary task for an educational constituency. Conflict over this philosophy has not ended.

Baptist college administrators were slow in accepting BSU work on their campuses. I. J. Van Ness, then general secretary of the Sunday School Board, commented about how hard it had been to convince many Baptist college presidents to allow this new organization, particularly in view of the quick, positive response from state schools.

During the 1920s Baptist schools were academies for church-related volunteers, but as the decades came and went this type of student came to be the minority. The denominational colleges could no longer claim their past. They took their rightful place as liberal arts colleges whose philosophy was within the framework of the Christian faith.

Other facets of denominational education needed intensive study and research, such as: Is the aim of church-related institutions scholastic or spiritual? Is the status of these schools academic or ecclesiastical?

Other questions have bearing on the purposes of higher education peculiar for Baptist campuses. What are the qualifications for students' admittance? Would the requirements be their high academic standings, or would they just have to be members of families of prominent church people? Would the school seek to conserve the Christianity of the arriving student or would it have the courage to explore new ideas and knowledge concerning the faith? History seems to validate the latter and Baptists should honor the work of their denominational schools of higher education.

As these colleges and universities demonstrate they are academically sound, many students outside the realm of "the womb of the church" find their way to these schools. Because of these type students, as well as those nurtured by churches, there is a *raison d'être* for BSU to be a part of the cocurricular activity of these schools and students. Yet, BSU has never enjoyed the same status on Baptist campuses as in state-supported institutions.

It would be naive to assume that every professor who teaches outside the Bible departments of denominational colleges is prepared or interested in giving a Christian perspective to the subject matter. Since this should be the major emphasis the Christian college has, that of presenting Christ in the classroom, it must be admitted that many times the Baptist college is as far from being a Christian community as a state-supported school. Also, a naivete exists if one assumes that all students attend Christian schools because they desire a Christian atmosphere.

Therefore, reasons exist for Baptist Student Unions on Baptist campuses as elsewhere. They may be tailored differently, but the needs are the same. The addition of BSU does not entirely satisfy the question of the ultimate success of the philosophical concept of Christian higher education. The dilemma has existed for seventy-five years, particularly in relation to campus ministry. Optimists would hope a more sophisticated philosophy of Christian higher education would develop and a peculiar BSU program would become more functional for these schools. That was the hope in 1958.

CONCLUSION

In the early 1950s, students came in droves to Baptist Student Unions. They were no longer the homogenous eighteen- to twenty-two-year-old single people that campus religious leaders had in the foregoing three decades. Eight different categories of students on campus have been analyzed in this chapter to point out their diversity. Hastily planned programs emerged without much thought as to their validity; in other words, programs ran ahead of philosophical concepts. That was the basis for Keegan setting up commissions. Diversified students demanded a diversified yet unified philosophy that would care for each group.

Something else happened. The work of the commissions filtered to local campus leaders and solidified a vocation. The "cheerleader" and "spiritual coach" images were replaced with one of academically and theologically trained people as campus ministers. They were gaining respect not only on campus but also among those in church circles.

However, discussion must continue to show that state and Conventionwide student departments were expanding, also. The integration of student work on all levels had to be accomplished before a unified philosophy could be determined. The BSU diamond needed polishing.

A Firm-Based but Ambiguous Program
(Attempting Philosophical Unification)

"The times they were a' changin'." By the end of the 1950s, more and more the growing and maturing of Baptist campus ministry and directors of student ministries became evident. Growth demanded change not only in organization and program but also in relationships. State student departments were assuming more and more programming. Also, because of maturation on the state level, the Sunday School Board Student Department was suggesting less programming and doing more research and publication—becoming a "think tank." All this did not come about peacefully.

STATE STUDENT DEPARTMENTS

The developing feelings of state directors were emphasized by Udell Smith, then state student director of Louisiana, when he commented, "Where Dr. Leavell worked with what he had at the beginning, Dr. Keegan came into a situation in the middle of change. The various [state] student departments were taking on more responsibility, programs were expanded and more decisions made at the state level."[1]

The forming of the Southern Baptist State Student Directors Association in 1959 was an indication that state leaders were intent on changing the philosophy of student work. Chester Durham, then state director of Kentucky student ministries and a veteran leader of the state men remarked, "There was a need for a fellowship among state men where someone else's program was not emphasized. . . . The maturation of the work caused state directors to feel they were confident professionals."[2]

They had no place they could meet to discuss paramount concerns such as budgets, student center construction, qualifications, policies, or salaries for local campus personnel. Also, relationships needed to be developed with the Home Mission Board (HMB) because of the extensive use of students in short-term mission programs and projects. A corollary to these programs was how students could be used in new territory work. Lastly, there were state programs peculiar to each state, and they could not be publicized by any agency of the convention.

No secrecy surrounded the matter. In fact, Keegan, when informed of the state director's intention to form an organization called the State Student Directors

Association, offered to subsidize the organizational meeting. In Louisville on May 18, 1959, this group was formed and held its first meeting in Baton Rouge, February 3–5, 1960. Durham was elected the first president, and Ralph Winders became the secretary.

The change was not harmonious, but the national staff members in Nashville were caught because of Sunday School Board philosophy. Those who determined Sunday School Board policy tended to equate the Student Department with the Sunday School and Training Union Departments. This view was untenable since student work was only church related—not church centered.

Over the years this new organization provided many benefits both for themselves and for those at the Sunday School Board, at the mission agencies, and on the local level. Emery Smith, state student director in South Carolina, summed it up best: "We have been the sounding board, the catalyst, the 'watch' dog, the motivator, the implementor, and the supporter of BSU—State, SBC, and worldwide."[3]

Although there were many concerns from the new state directors' association, summer missions and new territory work was the place where this group gave the most emphasis. These two endeavors would actually become "hand in glove" and provide the most distinct emphasis in the expanding program of BSU for the next four decades.

STUDENT MISSIONS

Courts Redford, executive director of HMB during the 1940s, has dated the beginning of student summer missions with the request in 1942 of W. W. Hamilton, president of the Baptist Bible Institute in New Orleans. Hamilton asked for financial assistance to certain students who served during the winter in the practical work department, but had no provision for employment during the summer. In a positive response to this request these students did mission work among the French Acadians in Louisiana during summer months. They were employed for four months and paid a stipend of thirty-five or forty dollars per month.

An interesting note is this type of work, performed a century earlier, predated all that Baptists attempted. Marianna C. Brown in discussing American Sunday School movements noted in 1901:

> The department of "student work" has been in operation from 1850 to 1860, but was discontinued for want of funds, and was not renewed until 1897.
> . . . Those who worked the first summer reported fifty-five Sunday Schools organized, one hundred and eighty-nine teachers, and sixteen hundred and twenty-five scholars.

These missionary students are advised to explain the work of the Union at the Gospel Meetings which they hold, and to take up an offering for it. The money so obtained must be reported to the Society, but the student is authorized to retain as his own, in compensation for his services, a sum not to exceed $30 for each month spent in the work.[4]

Also, Jane Young Poster has given insight into a different nature of summer work in her history, *Reckless for Christ*—a story of South Carolina's student program. Amidst the doldrums of the depression, Frank Leavell challenged students from Mississippi and South Carolina in 1932 to use ten-minute speeches written by denominational leaders to emphasize different aspects of the Cooperative Program. Leavell predicted, "It is possible that from this movement . . . there may come a spirit and a vigor that will help Southern Baptists to lift themselves from the depths of depression and financial embarrassment in which they now find themselves."[5]

However, it was William Hall Preston, associate Southwide secretary to Leavell, whom most Baptists consider the grandfather of campus ministries' summer missions. For several years he had spoken on various occasions about the possibility of using students in various ways during the summer—helping with Vacation Bible Schools, revival teams, and surveys for new churches to name a few. Finally, he took advantage of the youth revival phenomenon in Texas. A group of Baylor students went to Hawaii in 1947 and conducted an extremely successful evangelistic campaign. At the time no one realized that this was beginning the fulfillment of Preston's dream of utilizing hundreds and, ultimately, thousands of students for short-term mission service—not only summer but around the year.

In 1951 the Conventionwide Student Department agreed to send workers supported by various local Baptist Student Unions. This was a joint plan with all the mission boards involved. By the summer of 1960, Baptist Student Unions sponsored seventy-five home and sixty-two foreign missionaries.

To reiterate, summer missions program would probably become the most significant of all the new programs that student work would devise beginning in the fifties. From the brier patch of BSU came the foundation for Southern Baptists' program of Bold Mission Thrust to be culminated in 2000.

Summer mission's primary purpose in the beginning was *not* to secure more missionaries but to create a mission consciousness among all students. As John Irwin had observed of the past in his book *The Missionary Education of Young People,* the organization of exclusively missionary societies makes many people draw the conclusion that they can take their Christianity either with or without missions. Particularly among the boys and young men has been the tendency to regard missions as women's business.

The summer mission program negated this philosophy among Baptist students. The program was for all participants and not just members of Young

Women's Auxiliary. This activity launched the idea that missions was for the rank and file; that it was not an elective—an extra or a spiritual luxury for a few. Its primary purpose, well-intentioned, was achieved; however, a vast number of students felt God's calling to religious service changed their first-intended vocations and entered graduate work at various seminaries.

The activity of Courts Redford and W. W. Hamilton working together with students during the summer of 1942 dated the beginning of more and more specialization in terms of this embryonic idea. Many good reasons prevailed for students to serve God during the summer, but one of the most significant considerations may have been overlooked. Summer service was a unique opportunity to explore the reality of other occupations and aspirations. It proved to be a major factor in influencing young lives toward church-related vocations; it educated those who were destined to be church leaders to see missions as a major emphasis in church life.

As far as Southern Baptist agencies were concerned, summer mission work was the incubator for volunteerism on larger and various levels: Did not the ideas for Missionary Journeymen of FMB and the US-2 program (two-year program) of the HMB come from the results of summer missions? Or semester missions? Then somebody mused, "Why not ask for *adult* volunteers?" They could build new churches, repair mission centers, and be Campers on Mission. In 1994 the volunteer departments of HMB reported more than forty thousand people used in the programs mentioned and in other ways—all because of what started a half-century ago with students working during the summer.

NEW TERRITORY STUDENT WORK

With the advent of the Thirty Thousand Movement, which called for additional missions and churches throughout SBC plus the expansion of HMB into the Northeast, Midwest, and West, the Conventionwide Student Department began efforts to organize students in these areas. Philosophy and ways had to be projected in order to determine who was going to be responsible for the work. Another crucial matter was how to combat the inevitable charge of encroachment from other denominations already in these areas.

H. Eugene Maston, formerly BSU director at McNeese State University in Lake Charles, Louisiana, resigned in the latter part of the 1950s and became what was then known as a "pioneer" BSU director. (Originally this whole program of expansion was called "pioneer work.") He initially went to the University of Chicago and while completing a master of arts degree at that institution inaugurated a BSU program in the city. Afterward, Maston entered Columbia University to study for his doctorate in philosophy. Here he started work with students in conjunction with the Northeastern Baptist Association, a Southern Baptist group. The combining of graduate study with establishing BSU groups became the norm for the coming years. Maston did much to establish the philosophy that would become that of the Sunday School and Home Mission Boards.

Maston admitted that it was a fair question to ask why Southern Baptists were in these areas. By emphasizing three points, he formulated the philosophy of student work in new territories over the nation. He wrote that Southern Baptists being in the Northeast did not say that no one else had or was presenting the gospel to students in that area. The number of nonchristian students was so great and the laborers so few, he said, that it behooved all evangelical Christians to do as much as they could to meet their spiritual needs—whether they be Southern Baptists or not.[6]

Because more students from the South were beginning to seek higher degrees than the baccalaureate, someone needed to accept responsibility, if church conservation was still important, to care for these wandering Baptists. This became Maston's second emphasis. The third emphasis also represented the old traditional philosophy of encouraging students' spiritual maturation as intelligent Christians.

Maston concluded following:

> These three, then, are the fundamental purposes we have in mind as we began BSU here: enlistment of Southern Baptist students; leading these students in continuing spiritual growth; and missionary outreach among the many non-Christians among us. Only when these have been considered is there room for such important, but secondary, purposes as fellowship and Christian social life.[7]

Despite the obvious traditional purposes, one of the first new territory directors of student ministries recognized that the approach to these types of students needed to be *different* from that in the South. The old slogan of BSU being a link between the church and campus wasn't going to be as prevalent in these areas of the nation. There were enormous numbers of students who had no religious affiliation; therefore, evangelistic efforts came to be paramount. The work took on mission-field characteristics—the groups were small.

Different also meant recognizing that the mores of the South should not be carried to these areas. This was the major weakness not only of student work but also of the whole new territory program of expansion among Southern Baptists. What happened in Arkansas churches, for example, wasn't necessarily what *should* happen in the Northeast, Midwest, or West. The mobility of Southern Baptists after World War II was the foundation of most new programs and churches that carried the baggage of "no dancing, card playing, smokin' or chewin'." Actually, churches were founded on mores—Southern ones—and not on New Testament doctrine alone. The natives of these regions, for the most part, viewed Baptists of the South a little above snake handlers. Fortunately, as the years became decades, this view changed, though slowly.

David K. Alexander was chosen in July 1961 to assume the reins of the Conventionwide Student Department. As usual, many tasks were left to do at the death of Keegan. Not only was the unification of the philosophy of student work in progress, but also action on new convention philosophy needed to be developed. The Sunday School Board announced in 1962:

> David K. Alexander . . . announced that ten university campuses selected for half-time workers or graduate student scholarships are the Universities of Chicago, Colorado, Kansas, Michigan, Oregon, and Wyoming; also Ohio State, Purdue, and Utah State Universities. An appreciable portion of each worker's time will be devoted to international students.

> Los Angeles and New York City will get full-time workers. . . . The worker in NYC will also work with the cadets at the United States Military Academy.

> The placement of Baptist Student Union directors at the United States Air Force Academy . . . and the Naval Academy . . . resulted from a co-operative arrangement between the Sunday School Board and the Home Mission Board where the Sunday School Board underwrites the worker's salary and operating expenses for half his time spent in the ministry to cadets (or midshipmen) and faculty members, and the Home Mission Board and State Executive Boards pay for the other half of his time to be spent in a ministry to military personnel in the surrounding area.[8]

This long quote is important because the words became the philosophy through which both agencies have cooperated for almost a half-century. Some details have changed through the years; however, this effort has grown more than any of the instigators dreamed. HMB's US-2 program was launched almost concurrently.

During the early 1960s, a few US-2 appointees had been assigned responsibilities in areas where a major part of their time was given to student work. Although they were not appointed as BSU directors but as associate pastors or youth directors in nearby campus churches, they were actually campus ministers with accountability to the local or state mission supervisor and not to the state BSU director or the Sunday School Board. This plan was begun under the administration of Warren Woolf, then director of the present Special Ministries Department of HMB.

The Sunday School Board Student Department and HMB entered this new arena during the time of total expansion in student work and have challenged Baptist students to serve outside the traditional South. In the beginning volunteers—faculty members, church workers, or pastors—started the program. This is another example of the evolution that has been evident since the early history of BSU. Pioneer work outside the South was part of an expanding BSU program following World War II.

CHANGES IN EDUCATION

Maturation of state programs and the expansion of student work into new territorial areas were not the only reasons that a more unified philosophy needed to be developed. Changes in education had been taking more and more of center stage. Higher education has always been a factor in American society, but at no time has its role been more influential than the beginning of the seventh decade of the twentieth century.

Several factors, or shifts, had become more than just noticeable:

In 1950 there were about 2.2 million undergraduates; in 1965 there were about 5.4 million undergraduates. The total number had more than doubled in a mere decade and a half.

This was becoming the age of the great university complexes; at the same time, community colleges were appearing in almost every county seat.

Though 40 percent of American colleges had some form of religious affiliation, enrollments in those were decreasing while state-supported institutions were increasing. Private colleges were also losing students.

Both faculty members and students had become more mobile.

Students preferred urban colleges and universities.

Negro colleges' future had begun to look unfavorable.

Coeducation was gaining in relation to all-men's and all-women's institutions.[9]

Overall, these factors, or shifts, caused Christian students to lose identity with the university as community. If they were related to any campus group, it was likely a professional one, not a social or religious one. Also, student services were greatly extended. Well-staffed counseling facilities, infirmaries, and dining halls made the early 1960s campuses more and more self-sustaining. This meant that less and less did students' lives relate to "town" communities, including the church.

Finally, the most important factor during this era was the changing student. The old caricature of college as those days of "having a lark" were over. These students were there for the primary aim of studying. Twenty-six percent of the national student body were married. An increasing number were graduate students, and thousands of internationals were enrolled. The emerging world was part of the everyday experience of these collegians. So the Commission on Married Students challenged new program planners with a startling statement:

The question for the church is this: Might not all these circumstances indicate something to the church and its campus ministry, particularly the ministry whose main emphasis is on a weekly fellowship meeting directed at single undergraduate students living in campus residences? Being relieved of providing social and recreational opportunities . . . the church may now be free for a mission of extraordinary significance?[10]

The times were a' changin'!

CAMPUS AND CHURCH AS COMMUNITY

As stated in chapter 2, campus ministry in its beginnings was often seen as a counteraction for the "godless" university believed to be conducted by subchristian standards, Verlyn L. Barker, then secretary for campus ministry of the United Church of Christ observed:

The expectations of these ministries have often been to preserve the students "by protecting and guarding them from the corrosive acids of rationalism." . . . Stated differently, campus ministry has been seen as a program in which the "religious" part of man is nourished even as the university cares for the intellectual, physical, and social needs of the individual. Too often the view has been that, since those in public institutions were not so fortunate as to be able to attend a church-related school, or not wise enough to choose one, the next best course was to follow them.[11]

Churches could no longer see their responsibility simply as providing activities in student centers or foundation houses. Campus ministers saw the day passing, just because of campus secularization, that concerned Christians belonged in the "midst of the action." The time had come to raise the question: If universities claimed to offer a universal curriculum, yet omitted theological disciplines, how could they avoid the accusation of multiversities? Cardinal John Henry Newman long ago in his brilliant book, *The Idea of a University*, raises the very question. This was the crucible of community.

Therefore, the relation between church and higher education should have been *one* between communities of persons rather than *two* separate entities. If these communities of people do have a common relationship to Christianity, then Southern Baptists were obliged (and still are today) to continue their search with higher education to become one.

The Christian faith needed to permeate the academic community if the church of the future was to provide leadership for a whole person in a fragmented world. Again, Verlyn Barker spoke during this era, "The day for the recreational leader and the popularizer of the faith has gone forever; the day has arrived when the church must raise up men [sic] who can participate in the battle of ideas."[12]

As an aside, those men and women from denominations other than Southern Baptists and Roman Catholics who perpetuated these same true maxims were to choose the wrong road to solve this important question. The ecumenism of all groups besides those mentioned began in the 1960s, and their students were ignored in the process. Consequently, their idea of "saving the university" was the death knell of their student work as it had been known historically. Ecumenical programs involving their students dwindled significantly. The beginning of taking away funds for these groups could have possibly resulted from their denominational leaders being displeased with the new philosophical route their campus leadership was taking. That did not mean, however, that Southern Baptists did not need to wrestle with the idea that ignoring the study of religion by the university made it a "multiversity."

TOWARD PHILOSOPHICAL UNIFICATION

Recognizing the changing role of state student departments, the inserting of the vast program of student missions coupled with Southern Baptists going into new territories (making it a national denomination), and the realization that fragmented BSU programs were trying to reach a diversified student body, the Conventionwide Student Department in its 1960 report to that SBC stated that student work is designed to discover, develop, and promote principles and methods for the enlistment of students in the work of the churches and to enlarge and improve the Baptist witness to the campus.[13]

This was a progress report rather than a description of a completed task. The six commissions formed in 1958 were still studying all phases of campus ministry programs. The overall commission had the dubious title "Commission on Expansion." Its purpose was to define a basic objective, and/or objectives, for the Baptist Student Unions of the convention. They were to report the next summer at the annual BSU directors meeting in Nashville.

The Commission on Expansion

The 1958 Commission on Expansion noted trends in philosophy of education that were affecting student religious work. Two tendencies were the desire to provide educational opportunities for every person and the development of more and larger colleges and universities of a nonsectarian nature. Another was the initiation of the age of space, which tended to make science the most important discipline and make classroom work more serious. This trend called for revitalization of Christian thought, especially in reference to religion and the Bible being taught as a part of a higher-education curriculum.

The changing philosophy of American education had its effect upon campus religious work. The demand for more mature leadership, for different types of workers, and consequently, a different type of ministry ensued. Members of the Commission on Expansion wrote in their report, "Our ministry is no longer limited to *students*, but includes faculty, administration, and staffs in the university center."[14]

Before conclusions were drawn or objectives made, the commission suggested further areas of study. The basic assumption was that expansion meant new organization. Pilot projects on certain types of campuses were a procedural means. More personnel for larger campuses, better training for leaders already there, internships for new personnel, refresher courses and sabbaticals—all these were considered as ways to examine a "new" campus ministry and minister.

From the premise of the changing educational philosophy and campus constituency with its effect on campus religious organizations and their leaders, the commission suggested the following objectives and procedures:

> The basic objective of Baptist Student Union is to lead each person of the academic community into a maturing Christian experience.
>
> To achieve this objective, each local BSU will develop methods and techniques to:
> 1. Encourage effective church membership (through training and experience in worship, stewardship, church organizations and activities).
> 2. Develop concern for evangelism and missions (through mission education and offerings, ministries to foreign students, witnessing to the unsaved, off-campus mission centers and activities, summer service opportunities).
> 3. Build stronger personal spiritual life (through prayer and Bible study, through campus organizations of special interests).
> 4. Train the members of the collegiate community for Christian leadership (through personal counseling, discussion groups, vocational and marriage guidance, Focus Weeks, study courses, Bible teaching).
> 5. Provide opportunities for Christian fellowship and recreation (through a student center and social activities).[15]

The committee presented its report at the conclusion of the 1959 Student Director's Conference in Nashville with the request they be allowed another year of additional study before making a final report.

It is immediately evident in the above work that this was only the use of techniques, or programs, to get to philosophical concepts. Keegan did not grant the request of a year's extension, perhaps because of its programmatic nature. There was another reason: state student directors had been asked to serve on the six commissions as only *ex-officio* members; they refused.

Therefore, to smooth the waters, the Conventionwide secretary appointed another group being called, for unknown reasons, "Study Group I." The members—four state directors and four local directors—of this committee worked faithfully to carry out its assignment. Its purpose was to evaluate Baptist campus ministry and to create a philosophy that would include the scope of the ministry and the objectives and terminology of student work.

A special issue of an early 1963 *Quarterly Review*, a convention publication basically for pastors and other staff personnel across the land, was devoted entirely to Southern Baptists' campus ministry:

> The philosophy, though concisely stated, gives the reason why the program of student work is needed. The philosophy influences the stating of the objectives which are common to the task of the Student Department of the Sunday School Board at the Conventionwide level, the state departments of student work, the local Baptist Student Unions, and the work of the churches which have students commuting from home to college daily.[16]

CONCLUSION: A PHILOSOPHY AND OBJECTIVES OF BAPTIST STUDENT WORK

In December 1962 twenty-eight state student directors met with the Sunday School Board Student Department staff on philosophy, objectives, and terminology. Slight revisions were made in the statement of objectives, but the statement of philosophy was adopted as presented in this work as Appendix A.

The report broadened educational and religious terminology. For instance, the word *witness* became everything a person is and does in the name of Christ, which certainly is New Testament evangelism. Although the words *student work* are ambiguous, they were an attempt to describe all that Baptists did in ministry to the academic community. Despite serious debate as to whether the ministry should include campus adults, the adopted philosophical statement did so; specifically, it included faculty, staff, and administrative personnel.

A philosophy of Christian education was described as the supposition that God is not only the source but also the revealer of all truth. This idea was further emphasized by the statement: The Christian perspective is essential to the realization of the ultimate purpose of higher education, the Christ-centered worldview that gives meaning and purpose to the process and product of education. This view is necessary to effect a reconciliation of the Greek—with the Christian concept of education.[17]

This definition of the nature of the university was strong and unique. It emphasized that the university involves individuals with high potential in a period of accelerated development. During this time there is also confrontation with verbal expression of conflicting ideas and values. As the student lives in the retreat of the ivory tower, each searches for his or her place in the world at large.

The reasons given for a specialized ministry, however, were shibboleths of the past. The role of the church was seen only through those in BSU who had relationships in the local expression of the body of Christ. The study group defined a specialized ministry as a program "to supplement and complement what we ordinarily do through the regular ministry of the church." As an after-thought, they did admit a wider mission of the church in stating its function as worship, proclamation, education, and ministry. Even this ambiguous statement did not give clear cognizance of the universal body of Christ's church.

The stated philosophy of Southern Baptist campus ministry was a strong attempt to develop a foundation for programming that had run wild in the 1950s. These commissions and the supplementing groups did an outstanding piece of work to create the firmest foundation since BSU's inception.

Now the task was to blend this statement—clear the ambiguities—with the work of agencies, state conventions, and local campuses, a process that would take many years. The road was twisted, curvy, and had many bumps. The outcome was the best and largest student program among the many denominations that saw academia as a mission field.

Toward Interpreting the Uncertainties
(Efforts to Blend Philosophy)

The decade of the 1950s has been described as "the bland leading the bland." Yet, revisionist David Halberstam argued in his book *The Fifties* that it was in that era the tumultuous sixties were fermented. No matter, the fifties was a great time to be a campus minister. Students and BSU blended.

Real family values—not the 1990s political varieties—and morality were inbred in arriving freshmen and religiously active upperclassmen. Solid, responsible, and invigorating spirituality described these students, who in later years would adopt views similar to Archie Bunker's. Everything in these years was black or white, no grays. If a campus minister said "jump," the 1950s' student would say, "how far?" No wonder, when the leader used the same words in the 1960s she/he was bewildered when the student asked, "Why?" Programs raced before philosophy.

Historians must credit Baptist campus ministry leadership on all levels for realizing this "helter-skelter" way of ministering could not continue. Some prophets among the group were feeling change in the incoming student even before the end of the decade of the 1950s they had so enjoyed. Thus the philosophical statement of 1962 was needed. The problem was how to handle the ambiguities that plagued every dimension of student work. The philosophical statement had to be more clearly defined. It might be wise to look at this time's ambiguity.

On the local scene the exciting *text* of success was evident. During the decade between 1950 and 1960 the number of local campus ministers nearly doubled: in 1950 there were 109 full-time local directors; in 1960 there were 190.[1] The *subtext*, which would last many years and may be continuous, was paradoxical or obscure to the text. Where was this organization leading?

AMBIGUITIES CONCERNING BAPTIST STUDENT UNIONS

If Baptist Student Unions were to minister to the total campus community, a new type of leader was needed. Historically, the BSU director had ministered almost totally to undergraduates. To shift suddenly to all-campus constituents was especially frustrating. Even the name, Baptist *Student* Union, was inadequate when the program expanded to include faculty and administration.

Also, there was no guarantee that a one-person staff had time or expertise to minister to all the types of people congregated on university campuses. No one person was likely to have adequate knowledge about graduate, international, or married students when his or her "world" had been undergraduates. The expansion of personnel seemed to be the answer, but what kind of educational preparation would they need? The Commission on Expansion was candid in observing that one of the reasons for rapid turnover in leadership was poor educational backgrounds. The members of this commission acknowledged the following:

> We may rationalize by saying that the B.S.U. movement is still relatively in its infancy, and therefore, we have not had enough time to work out standards of qualifications and preparation. A more palatable rationalization [is] the B.S.U. program has grown so much we have not been able to keep pace with the educational preparation and training needed for persons entering the field.[2]

The master's degree in religious education had been the prevalent one for directors of student ministries. It did not take long for these folk to realize that much they dealt with was theological. Other types of training suggested were sabbatical years or, at least, summer study. Internships became a vehicle used, in firmly established work, for those wanting to enter this area of religious service. All these ideas were to help solve the enigma of what a campus minister was as a person. At the same time, these suggestions were an attempt to create a lifelong profession.

One other idea, considered by other denominations although an anathema to Baptists, would have helped to clarify the ambiguity of the one-person staff. A "student" of student work should have been intrigued with the possibilities inherent in ecumenical ministries. For example, Robert Sanks, at that time co-director of the Wesley Foundation at the University of Wisconsin, commented concerning the married student:

> The married student "villages" may be served by campus Christian ministries dividing the responsibility on a geographical basis. In the geographical area, instead of a denominational area, Christians should join together to nurture their understanding of the faith, and in service to bear witness to the faith. It is an opportunity to dramatize the fact that Christian action and dialogue are concerns of the entire Christian parish.[3]

Though not widely known, a great amount of Baptist work has been done ecumenically, increasing in the early 1960s and mostly in what was called "city-wide" student work. In metropolitan areas—with many and various types of institutions—it was impossible that Baptist workers had the time or were qualified to deal with *every* situation. In New Orleans, for example, different denominational student ministers worked in unusual circumstances. One supervised the work at the medical centers; at Tulane University different clergy would be responsible for a "voice of faith" in specific dormitories, one of which housed athletes. Spiritual counseling in the university student center offices was staffed by each on scheduled days of the week. At the major commuting school, the University of New Orleans, the "expert" was available to the lives and work of those students facing another peculiar challenge. Finally, what was the needed response to the many fine Christian students of other denominations, some of them refugees from Campus Crusade and InterVarsity, who came to BSU centers looking for more mature ways to grow in the faith?

In spite of "Southern Baptistizing" (Walter Shurden's phrase), every work of this communion has always had a hidden agenda among the directors of student ministries of ecumenical participation. When Shurden, chair of the Christianity Department at Mercer University, wrote an updated history of the Baptist Sunday School Board in 1981, he stated that during the period (1917–1935) when I. J. Van Ness headed this organization, denominational loyalty was a guiding principle. In 1919 Van Ness initiated a Sunday called "Denominational Day" for the promotion of denominational principle and programs.[4] One needs to remember that Frank Leavell was a colleague of Van Ness and the first basic principle of BSU was "the work shall be frankly denominational."

All this points to the obscurity of what kind of religious vocational creature this campus person would be. Also, it pointed to the dubiousness in the philosophical statement of 1962. This statement was clearer when staffs increased and educational requirements and specialization were clearly defined.

AMBIGUITIES CONCERNING LOCAL CHURCHES

Assuming that both church and university must become partners in community, the stated philosophy contained the phrase: "The role of the churches is indispensable to the maturing spiritual, moral, and intellectual lives of students and faculty members."[5] To accomplish this, changes needed to be made in perceived church images of those in academia.

Deane William Ferm explained these paradoxical images by noting: The nature of the university with its tremendous freedom and variety, the differences in theological points of view, and the baffling problem of effective communication make for a complexity that is equaled only by its gravity.[6]

As much as this statement is true, there has to be a sense of wondering if incoming Baptist freshmen have any idea of the philosophical distance between the Athens of academia and Jerusalem of the church. A psychological barrier that new students face is that they look at student religious centers—and churches—and think two things, both bad: "Those people *are* just like the church at home, I do not want to go in there" or "Those people *are not* like the church at home, I do not want to go in there." Not until this student progresses through college classes and other curricular activities during these wonderful collegiate years does she/he begin to see negative images of the church and the presented faith. This is why the student minister's office may be the place where most significant spiritual pilgrimages begin and positive images of church and faith develop. What goes on in the "inner sanctum" may be entirely different from the program in the religious center. Both negative and positive images of the church should be faced and discussed if contributions to the Christian maturation of these "missionary" students are to be available.

Negative Images

First, church people at times seem gullible. Many arriving freshmen have had their fingers burned in the matters of religion. The home church did not prepare them for the varieties of philosophies and the cynicism of professors in the academic community. Therefore, the student has a tendency to make sweeping conclusions that all churches are gullible. The old answers—without interpretation to life—trust in God, read the Bible, and pray—have had their innings and struck out.

Second, if the first negative image is that the churches' answers are too easy, the next is that they are too rigid. The church has a tendency to reject what has been, in the past, one of its most cherished doctrines—individual freedom. If the church message is for every person, it must speak the language of "gown" as well as "town." True, there is no way that this is accomplished every day, or every Sabbath, but the spirit of God's people must have a persuasiveness of fresh air for open minds.

Also, a historical argument has been that collegians be allowed to worship on campus, not near campus. Such groups as United Methodists and Roman Catholics have nearly always had "church on campus." These arguments have been in some ways valid, in others invalid. There is a truism that campus churches can provide ministry specifically targeted for students by preaching to their particular needs each Sunday. On the other hand, much wailing by denominations other than Baptists about their church's young people not returning to local congregations after graduation has persisted.

Perhaps it is better to risk letting students find local churches that speak to them at this stage in life and hope that transition after university days will not be traumatic. In the 1990s a different question may arise: How does one get this "abandoned generation" back to church?

Last, the image of being socially conservative and insensitive may be the church's most devastating one. This image perhaps has done more harm to the faith than any other. One such crisis was the Civil Rights movement. At that time someone said, "The most segregated hour of the week is the eleven o'clock church hour." Today, there are new social issues to tackle, and there always will be. Will the churches be willing to struggle with these or will they bring up the rear as they too often did in the 1950s and 1960s?

Positive Images

With prayerful hope that the discussion concerning negative images is not too harsh, there are positive images for those in the academic community. There are churches on the horizon that simulate the following suggestions:

The church should appreciate and encourage honest doubt.

The church should be a teaching community of the highest order.

The church in the person of its minister should become involved as much as possible in college life.

The church should be concerned with issues that the students and faculty consider critical.

The church should educate its people to the meaning of theological terms and seek to translate terms in understandable idioms.

The church should be deeply sensitive to and involved in the social issues of today.

No one should ever question the mission opportunities for the church on the university campus. Here the leaders for the denomination, the nation, and the world are to be found. Here competing faiths meet head-on in a life-and-death struggle for the minds and hearts of both young people and adults. It is of vital importance, therefore, that the church approach this task with a sharpened intellect and dedicated heart. The local church minister has a responsibility but also a wonderful challenge. That was true as Southern Baptist student work tried to develop a unified philosophy in the early 1960s; it is true in the 1990s.

If the state philosophy of student work during this 1960s era was to become functional, it was obvious the church was to play a positive role. The day of one church in the academic community was no longer true; many Baptist churches now surrounded most colleges. The day when dormitory students arrived in September and did not return home until Thanksgiving was history—if for no other reason than mobility. (Some wag said, "The campus police are not allowing students but two cars in the future; the faculty cannot find places for their ten-year-old buggies.") The increase in daily commuters made almost every church a collegiate one, as concluded by Doyle Baird:

By now it should be obvious that the Baptist Student Union cannot "deliver" students to any specific church. The organization should not be thought of as merely a "pipeline" to be used to "funnel" students into the church. Enlistment in the churches continues to be a primary but not the only purpose of BSU. The emphasis in the organization must magnify and explain the church's role to students. Its leaders, by precept and example, must place great importance on responsible church membership.[7]

In summary, two developments in Southern Baptist life by the early 1960s put more responsibility on the churches to create positive images for the fertile minds in academe. The multichurch situation meant that more pastors were having to ask themselves if they had the training and the intellectual desire to cope with these ever-questioning youngsters. Pastors did not have a choice; students were in their pews each weekend. If God had placed a church in an academic setting, it was required that it minister to all congregants—even those in academia. The challenges were many and changing as those in the church faced the entrance of the sixties.

AMBIGUITIES CONCERNING STATE STUDENT WORK

At this time in BSU history there were two prominent areas that needed clarification. The denomination's program designs were not the same as those needed on the local level, and accurate job descriptions were lacking for local student workers and staffs.

On the whole, BSU state programs were those that had been a part of student programs since the 1940s—annual conventions, directors' meetings, spring retreats, and Ridgecrest Conference Center's conventionwide meeting for students in June. Program expansion on the state level still was designed to minister almost entirely to undergraduates. The exception was the states' ministry to internationals and that was in cooperation with the Sunday School Board Student Department. Although in the 1950s one-fourth of the students enrolled in college were married or graduate students, almost nothing was being done to encourage them to attend state meetings through program planning or in providing for their personal needs.

When the personnel on the state level finally provided job analyses for local campus staff members, the ambiguity of conventionwide philosophy cleared. No group was more aware of this than state student directors. Udell Smith of Louisiana reminded state directors in 1962 that "we are paramount in the selection of personnel . . .; we finance the program by raising budgets . . .; we construct student centers. . . ." In the speech, Smith said, "the fine art of policy making is our signal contribution," and emphasized that "every great student program is operated on sound policies and keen organization."[8]

The mature thinking of all state directors made tremendous strides in a vocation that was trying to become a lifelong process. Simultaneously, the stated philosophy of Southern Baptist student work was weaving itself into the fabric of BSU work.

AMBIGUITIES CONCERNING CONVENTIONWIDE AGENCIES

Perhaps the stated philosophy was most ambiguous in three vital convention agencies: HMB, the Education Commission, and the Education Division of the Sunday School Board of which student work was a department. The thesis of this section is not to intimate hostility, for there was none. It is to suggest murky waters needed clearing so the new philosophical statement would function to its fullest extent for the kingdom of God—henceforth called "the beloved community," a phrase coined by Martin Luther King Jr. that is more gender inclusive. By clearing waters, two accomplishments would be serving the best interest of students and, conversely, encouraging students to serve agencies to the fullest.

Baptist Home Mission Board

The SBC was no longer just a southern entity since the state convention of California was admitted to this group during the middle of this century and was quickly followed by other new state conventions. It did not take a prophet to see that ultimately the convention would become national in scope. This made a great impact on student work; suddenly, the majority of students in the United States were outside the "old convention territory."

Both the Conventionwide student department and the Atlanta HMB soon would begin to comprehend the value of a student summer mission program. Since 1944 students had been a target group of HMB to help in meeting this agency's objectives of church starting, church growth, ministry, and evangelism. The basis for cooperation between the two national agencies was written and agreed upon. The national student ministry office would be responsible for developing programs in "new territory" areas, and HMB would be responsible for personnel. Each Conventionwide agency was wise to see the great potential of these young people in reaching people for Christ and the Baptist witness.

By the 1990s the Ministry Division of HMB had expanded the idea of summer missions to include students who stayed longer periods of time at various assignments near college and university campuses. Short-term missionaries worked from one semester to two years. Volunteer student workers became members of the Mission Service Corps, raising their own expenses and serving as long as three or four years. Work teams, mainly construction, called SPOTS (Student Projects Other Than Summer) would go to many places to minister for approximately a week between semesters or during holiday periods.

Although many departments at the board used students, clearly the largest group was used by the Ministry Section. In 1989 Special Ministries had thirty-two career missionaries, and nineteen "US-2ers." Mission Service Corps had 113 volunteers with student work assignments; short-term student-work volunteers (semester missionaries) numbered 27.[9] This does not include approximately fourteen hundred students involved each summer. No one envisioned in the initial years of summer missions, except William Hall Preston "the father of summer missions," what actual possibilities existed. These successes illustrated how the stated philosophy became functional.

There were other interesting areas of HMB where students could help a unified philosophy to function, particularly in the area of evangelism. An underlying dilemma has pervaded Southern Baptist life since its inception: Should the initial encounter with the Christian faith be an integral part of every program or a separate "department" made up of people who give all their time to this endeavor? The answer is probably *both,* but a clear position should be taken as to the meaning implied. Organization for any part of the faith will ultimately demand partitioning. Evangelism is a part of the Christian life that flows among and through all the other parts of the faith. This is very important: those who give their lives to evangelism "departmentally" may unconsciously be trapped into a tendency to feel spiritually superior to colleagues in other areas of work which are also "departmentalized." Spiritual elitism is the hound of heaven that professional people in evangelism should constantly guard against.

College students need to heed the apostle Peter's admonition, "Always be ready to make your defense to anyone who demands from you an accounting for the hope that is in you" (1 Pet. 3:15, NRSV). Therefore, somebody in some department needs expertise in dealing with evangelism in academe.

In the early 1960s, HMB tried to provide that. Gray Allison was given the assignment in the Evangelism Department of HMB to devise evangelistic emphases particularly for students. The new stated philosophy of student work implied that evangelism was to be emphasized throughout Baptist student ministry, so Allison's work was a deviation from it. However, the intellectual element of the college community demanded deeper thoughts in order to give an accounting for the religious hope of Christian students.

One way Allison tried to put a new spin on collegiate evangelism was by helping directors of student ministries and students arrive at a satisfactory definition of evangelism for the college scene. Basically, the definition was one that included the whole spectrum of faith and not just the prevalent notion of an initial encounter with God through Christ. Also, knowledgeable people in the ways of student thought processes were assigned to prepare materials that dealt realistically with the campus scene. New approaches of lifestyle evangelism were explored, and work began with local and state BSU directors in the planning of special conferences on evangelism.

Allison laid a particular and unique foundation for students. They realized, as the Acts of the Apostles declared, "Ye are witnesses," not *if* or *perhaps,* but *are* witnesses. At the present time the Evangelism Section at HMB still works with collegians and singles in evangelistic emphases.

Ambiguities between HMB and the Baptist Sunday School Board Student Department were more functional than philosophical. The precaution for each was that duplication of effort be avoided. Present-day evidence shows that mutual agreements between these groups have provided many ways and many students to extend the beloved community nationally—and all this in just fifty years.

THE EDUCATION COMMISSION

In June 1964 the question that had plagued student work since its inception reared its head again: In what agency did work with students belong? Thus another ambiguity.

During this time all agency programs were being studied. The following resolution was passed at the annual meeting of the Education Commission:

> Please determine whether the student ministries are now administered by the most appropriate agency of the convention, the Education Commission . . . asks the SBC Executive Committee. In every other major denomination, except Southern Baptists, student work is under their education boards. The Education Commission of the Southern Baptist Convention was chartered to handle all matters related to higher education.[10]

Long ago Leavell emphasized student work as a missionary task, while the Education Commission was founded upon the basis of academic and curriculum development. (There was no reason that the same could not be said at this juncture in history.) Yet, a continued attempt by the Education Commission to assume responsibility for the total area of Baptist higher education persisted. This contention divided the educational program of Southern Baptists to the detriment of both groups.

The program statement of the Education Commission only added credence to Leavell's observation that the commission was about academic and curriculum development:

> The Education Commission shall assist the Southern Baptist Convention in the propagation of the Gospel by . . . conducting varied services to enable schools and colleges to function more in the affairs of the denomination, and maintain a higher degree of efficiency in their educational undertakings. Pursuit of this objective should be the conviction that Baptist interest should be served in Baptist schools and colleges, under Baptist ownership and control, and supported all or in part by Baptists tithes and offerings.[11]

This sentence shows better than any other argument that only denominational education was the commission's concern. The background and history of this commission point to Baptist education as its only task.

During that period, and ever since, the commission's task has been fourfold:
1. A program of Christian education leadership and coordination is purported through publications such as the *Southern Baptist Educator* and the *Southern Baptist Campus Directory.*
2. The commission carries on an extensive program of Baptist college studies and surveys.

3. This group has a teacher recruitment and placement bureau for Baptist colleges.

4. The commission gives assistance in every area of Baptist college recruitment.[12] The work of the commission is only for the purpose of extending the philosophy of Baptist higher education.

A program of Christian education leadership and coordination is purported through publications such as the *Southern Baptist Educator* and the *Southern Baptist Campus Directory.*

The purpose here is not to disparage the work of the Education Commission because it played a vital role in the development and progress of Southern Baptist higher education. The purpose is to seek a solution to a problem that has too long been a source of dissension and has tended to fragment segments of Baptist constituents.

Unfortunately, most of the dissension had come from administrators of Baptist colleges. As has been reviewed, Van Ness was among the first to show cognizance of this as early as 1926. There were several reasons for this attitude:

1. As Baptist Student Unions developed they were viewed as competition because not only were they Christian alternatives but also state institutions were less expensive.

2. Baptist Student Unions cut into Cooperative Program educational dollars, and Baptist college administrators seemingly felt that this new state-supported entity was taking their money.

3. Educational philosophy of denominational schools, which may have been the work of their public relations people, left the impression that Baptist students in state schools were second-class citizens.

4. Christian educators looked upon BSU programs as an auxiliary one which did not get to the heart of Christian education.

Of all the reasons to question the validity of these new organizations on state campuses, the last one was the most true. However, again, Leavell was among the first to say BSU was a mission organization—not one of Christian education. It may have been a type of Christian education, but it did not fulfill a philosophical concept.

In the middle 1990s, this question still needs to be clarified. Trying to synthesize the philosophies of the work of Baptist colleges and student ministry is untenable. If BSU is wholly a missionary task then perhaps it should be a part of HMB. That has been the most prevalent suggestion over the past three decades. Until the Education Commission broadens its duties to other groups besides Baptist colleges, the work of campus ministry does not belong with them.

One solution may be a Department of Christianity and Higher Education under the Executive Committee of SBC, with an executive secretary over one director of Denomination Education and one director of Southern Baptist student work. Everyone should recognize the separate streams of two important programs.

Educators need to consider the plausibility of refraining from creating negative images and pursue the positive factors of both denominational education and student work—with the assumption both are worthy.

All of this discussion may truly be historical if the Restructuring Committee of 1995 has its way. Their primary goal is to downsize SBC's nineteen agencies to fourteen. The Education Commission is to be eliminated. Leaders will have to wrestle again where Southern Baptists' campus work belongs. The three-decade and continuing discussion will be renewed in whether this missionary endeavor should be under the new North American Mission Board.

Perhaps one should listen again to the words of Penrose St. Amant at the time the Education Commission asked for yet another study:

> Christian education is a community—involving the home, the church, the Baptist Student Union, the school, the college, the university—centered in Jesus Christ.

> Christian education gives man new vistas, wider horizons, and a purpose to use his gigantic powers. It provides him with a unifying perspective. As someone has said, "The course of study goes to pieces because there is nothing to hold it together. Triviality and mediocrity take over because there is no standard by which to judge them." Well, as Christians our standard is clear. It is Jesus Christ Who is Lord of all, and therefore, also of our minds.[13]

CONCLUSION

Adin Steinsaltz in his book *Biblical Images* observed that history is full of big fathers who leave no room for their sons to prove themselves. He was writing of Abraham and the difficulties of his sons to carry the burden of the promises of God to make a great nation. The same could have been said of those second generation sons and daughters who followed father Leavell in BSU.

Second generation people also faced formidable objective forces and circumstances. Ambiguities always have had a tendency to exist in efforts to broaden and make current a first generation movement—so with new philosophies.

The text of the campus movement in the 1950s was a wildly successful program moving along with little knowledge as to its ultimate goals, though numbers of students were participating. At the same time, a subtext was an undercurrent to plan for the only God-known future of Baptist campus ministry. That subtext was a new stated philosophy. The second generation unplugged old wells as they contemplated a bright new future. What this second generation did not know was that other and different wells were going to be dug for the tumultuous 1960s.

The Nation at Adolescence—The Age of Aquarius
(Christian Faith as Catalyst)

The dualism—the physical apart from spiritual—of ancient Greece is severely challenged with the spiritual and physical synthesis of Jewish religious life. The incarnation of God in Jesus of Nazareth hails salvation to anyone who believes. Initial salvation is only the locomotive to the Christian train. Testing the validity of the "train" is asking the question "What does Christ have to say about every area of life from birth to death?"

For an adolescent nation in the 1960s and early 1970s this question became imperative. Consequently, simple salvation as the key to life's questions was no longer viable. If Christ was the answer, what were the questions? The 1950s' utopia was slaughtered with the advent of the soaring sixties.

There was something in the air! As important as the rapid growth of Baptist Student Unions was, as important as the struggle to make a statement of philosophy work—there was something else in the air. The American psyche was perhaps tested in this century as it had not been since Revolutionary days.

The nation's adolescent years were to begin with similar problems of individual adolescence. Christian faith was challenged but would be a catalyst to the coming lifestyle of the 1960s. On college campuses across the nation Baptist Student Unions would be vehicles to prove faith functioned in chaotic times. There was something in the air.

A SHORT LOOK AT TWO DECADES

Jeffrey Hart, a professor at Yale, in his book *When the Going was Good!* wrote that some pundits put the exact date of a new era, which would last more or less two decades. It began June 6, 1944—D-day—when General Eisenhower said three words, "Well, we'll go." And, *GO!* America did with all the raging orchestra of hormones found in budding adolescents.

From the time individuals returned from war-torn Europe and Asia, the Great Depression was a bad memory. Once "having seen Paree" they were not going to stay on the farm, nor in the home town of yesteryear. Mobility was the new word and President Eisenhower's 1956 U.S. Interstate Act made for everyone's mobility. (Most people have forgotten that this act was primarily for military purposes.)

Many stereotypes of the 1950s do not stand up to rigorous examination, but all contain a kernel of truth. Air-conditioning for those in the southern United States practically guaranteed a New South. One newfangled medium was a contraption to behold! The advent of television came at a time of stable values in families, homes, and country. (The argument continues as to what this form of media has done to the 1950s values of the nation.) Those of the silent generation did not realize how it would change society. *GO!* Americans did. They had not seen prosperity since the decade of the 1920s when, as historian Paul Johnson concluded, America had lost utopia.[1]

The bad old days were present, also. Rumblings out of Russia about communism's ultimate takeover only increased hysteria with the advent of Sputnik. This alone changed the higher educational scene from the traditional liberal arts environment to a chaotic rush to science buildings. Winston Churchill's "Iron Curtain" speech in Fulton, Missouri, in 1956; John Foster Dulles's "brinkmanship" foreign policy; and the nation's working to stockpile atomic weapons all caused historians to wonder if the latter years of the sixth decade of the century weren't the closest the world ever came to nuclear disaster.

Free speech was not so free in the 1950s. Loyalty oaths prevailed. The House Un-American Activities Committee, chaired by Martin Dies, coupled with the ravings of Senator Joseph McCarthy, kept citizens looking around every corner for a communist. The 1954 school desegregation laws brought about White Citizens' Councils and every evil that racial fears bring. Christians were forced, because of their following of the Galilean, to choose where they stood. Gallant people found the consequences of following Christ.

Was the 1950s citizen part of a more moral nation when legalized segregation prevailed; when women were denied equal opportunity; when people were punished because of their political beliefs and associations? Trying to abolish these gross abuses in so short a time as two or three decades was arguably the greatest moral advance this nation experienced. It must be admitted, however, a lot of the attempts were adolescent in nature. The notion that the United States is a less moral nation today than it was in the 1950s is a monument to historical revisionism.

One tends to agree, however, with the contents of several books—one is Bill Morris's *Motor City*—when they suggest that the 1950s planted the seed for the turbulent 1960s. With the election of John F. Kennedy, the first president born in the twentieth century and the first Roman Catholic to grace the White House, America was experiencing the first feelings of puberty.

By the end of the sixth decade some people began to wonder if the coming generation of young people would be different. A subconscious uneasiness and nervousness seemed to undermine the solidity everyone had felt since the end of World War II.[2] Thousands of words—spoken through television, magazines, and books—analyzed the paralysis caused by the generation gap. As the 1960s dawned, students became more promiscuous. Sexuality and drug addiction were preludes to the "hippie" generation that was willing to place any blame on their parents. Some theologians were saying that God was dead; they abdicated their role as signposts to God and assumed the role of last prophets. There was not only a new theology but also a new morality.

This entire decade probably could be summarized by three events: racial integration, Vietnam, and, strangely, the year 1968. Racial equality gradually, if not grudgingly, became a part of America's landscape. The Vietnam War was this nation's longest and its most monstrous mistake. The year 1968 was the culmination of all the decadence of the decade.

Racial Integration

The 1940s had seen students timidly asking questions about the separation of blacks from whites, but even in Christian student organizations the discussions were mostly rhetorical. The breakthrough for black-white relations came during the 1950s, years that would cost some Baptist student directors their jobs.[3] Many were threatened by late-hour hate telephone messages and weekly hate mail from white supremacists. Black students became a part of many Baptist Student Unions; it was in the 1950s that more black students would participate than the decades that followed.

After August 1963 when Martin Luther King Jr. made his "I Have a Dream" speech at the Washington Memorial, the overt racial issue became less volatile, though an unsettled one. Who could forget his eloquent plea: "I have a dream my four little children will one day live in a nation where they will not be judged by the color of their skin but by the content of their character"?

Vietnam

Vietnam arrived in the American mind like some strange hallucination. This bizarre catastrophe shattered so much of the country's life—pride, faith in government, the ideals of adulthood—that even now the damage cannot be completely assessed. When the country revived from its coma in the mid-1970s, it was further stunned. Americans did a humanly understandable thing: they suppressed the memory of Vietnam.

Veterans came back from Asia wondering where their parade was. The politicians had sold them a bad bunch of goods. They were the first to fight not only a teenage war but also a losing one. That was the difference from previous military excursions—individuals had all come back to these shores previously as conquering heroes. Sometime between the Tet offensive and the last helicopter off the U.S. embassy roof, America threw away the social contract and left military people to straggle back into society as best they could.

Almost all this could have been predicted. Early in the Kennedy administration discontent arose. The escalation of something more than "advisors" caused an undercurrent and rumbling in the bellies of Americans, especially those most likely to be affected—many students. France had failed with the same endeavor decades before; why would America be successful? Communist containment was not as easy as keeping dominos from falling. America had not realized it was now "a nation among nations" and not the "policeman for the world."

College campuses were the seedbeds of discontent. Frankly, the discontent was not all altruistic—many students wanted to avoid the draft. This war was fought by minorities of the United States: African Americans, Hispanics, non-educated whites, and "grunts" (military regulars). Molly Ivins, the Fort Worth *Star-Telegram* columnist, recalled only five Harvard men were killed in Vietnam.

Directors of student ministries were challenged as never before as they dealt with the quandaries and dilemmas of virtuous living in times like these. On top of dealing with racial issues, they now had an unpopular war not only on faraway shores but on the local turf of campus communities.

1968

The year 1968 shaped a generation. More than a quarter of a century has passed since the tragedies, triumphs, and trivialities that prompted Abbie Hoffman to sarcastically declare "1968 was a great, wonderful year. They don't make years like that anymore." However, historian William L. O'Neill wrote that the nation seemed to be coming apart; so did Ronald Johnson, professor of American history at Georgetown University in Washington. Johnson was a modern-day Gabriel who intoned in the play *Green Pastures,* "Lord, is it time for me to blow? Everything nailed down is comin' loose!"

In passing, the nation seems to have come full circle since that fateful 1960s year. The rise of conservatism in nearly every life arena, with controversies in various denominations and politics, caused the election of Ronald Reagan and was the ultimate reaction to the radicalism that began in the 1960s. Now, partially in reaction to Reaganism, the nation is back to a modified liberalism. From disintegrating under a Democratic administration in 1968, the country was back in 1991 to electing a Democrat in an effort to come together again.

A year of searing images was 1968. *Time's* "Facts on File" shared the following events the magazine considered important:

January 30	Viet Cong and North Vietnamese launch Tet offensive.
February 12	Eldridge Cleaver's autobiography *Soul on Ice* is published.
March 12	Eugene McCarthy wins 42 percent of the vote in New Hampshire primary.
March 31	President Johnson announces he will not seek reelection.
April 4	Martin Luther King Jr. is assassinated in Memphis.
April 23	Students at Columbia University take over college buildings.
June 6	Senator Robert F. Kennedy is assassinated in Los Angeles.
June 19	Poor People's March on Washington takes place.
August 20	Soviet tanks roll into Czechoslovakia.
August 26–29	Riots at Democratic National Convention in Chicago occur.

October 12–27   Summer Olympic Games are held in Mexico City. U.S.
                 sprinters Tommie Smith and John Carlos raise fists in
                 black-power salute during playing of the national anthem
                 at medal ceremony.
November 5   Richard Nixon is elected president.
December 24–25   Apollo 8 circles the moon.

This list showed the establishment had changed since 1968, as well as racial
turmoil, the effects of Vietnam, and the results of adolescent chaos.[4]

No one would have dreamed that one more event would be the last gasp of the
closing era. The killing of four students, May 4, 1970, 12:35 P.M., at Kent State
University in Ohio meant that Vietnam had come home. The naivete of a nation
took flight in face of those students' deaths. Kent State epitomized the legacy of
idealism that had fermented for the previous decade.

Despite books that attempt to expose a different view of the 1960s such as
Peter Collier's and David Horowitz's *Destructive Generation: Second Thoughts about
the Sixties,* Americans tend to forget about those who sacrificed on behalf of the
less fortunate, those who gave their time and money to battle social injustice.
These authors seem to want to rob the young of this era where they dreamed and
were idealistic. All adults should remember they, too, had their utopias in youth.
What adult doesn't remember thinking just as idealistically when young as did the
youth of the sixties?

To be sure, after students achieved what were their "moral victories," they
developed more the ideals of their parents. Those who did not have low draft
numbers were not among those rioting on campus. Those who demanded to be on
faculty committees soon found themselves absent from this work even as were
their adult counterparts. Those who raved with McCarthy and McGovern were
soon voting Republican. The issues were more traumatic during this decade than
they were in the years when today's grandparents emerged from adolescence. The
accomplishments of the 1960s made the world stand up and notice.

THE CHRISTIAN FAITH AS CATALYST

Before anyone looks at the Christian faith's place in this era, he/she must at
least consider a parenthetical reflection upon the Jesus Movement. Others talked
or wrote about the Jesus freaks.

This phenomenon was a youth movement, but specifically not a student one.
It was a counteraction to attempt a correction to the present decade's decadent
activities among the youth of the land. Although student religious organizations
were not in its mainstream, some were affected on the fringes. On the whole for
campus groups, it was detrimental. (Why must the pendulum always swing from
one extreme to the other?)

Maureen Orth, a newspaper reporter who wrote extensively of the Jesus Movement, observed in a "Last Supplement" to the *Whole Earth Catalog,* "The first thing I realized was how different it is to go to high school today. Acid trips in the seventh grade, sex in the eighth, the Vietnam war a daily serial on TV since you were nine, parents and school worse than 'irrelevant'—meaningless. No wonder Jesus is making a comeback."[5] Men like Richard Hogue, Arthur Blessitt, and Bill Glass, the Baylor football All-American and former All-Pro Cleveland Brown linebacker, were evangelists who capitalized on the spiritual vacuum of the sixties.

The Jesus Movement had beginnings as early as 1967 and mainline groups were a part of what became an ecumenical process. Pentecostals, Roman Catholics, and some Southern Baptists were involved. The most prominent Baptist, perhaps, was the then youthful, thirty-seven-year-old pastor of First Baptist Church, Houston, John Bisagno. Walker L. Knight, then editor of Southern Baptists' *Home Missions* magazine was one of the first to recognize something unusual was happening. He and his staff were quick to write, reflect, and prophesy about the Jesus people.

Knight described movement expressions well when he wrote, "Movements have a way of being future oriented, whereas institutional expressions . . . usually are dedicated to conserving the values of the forces which gave them birth. This is another aspect of the eschatological emphasis of the present awakening [The Jesus Movement]. The emphasis is not on what God has done, but on what he is now doing."[6] He saw something new in this phenomenon.

The Jesus people had all the characteristics of other great awakenings, such as George Whitfield's in the eighteenth century and the China Shantung revivals of the early 1930s. Three facets seemed to have always been present: Jesus' love, the Holy Spirit, and the eminent return of the Lord. These brought about unrestrained religious enthusiasm that had filled vacuums of times past and now countered the secularism of this decade.

Even religious ethics were making a recovery—but not completely. Blessitt reported a streetwalker in New York told him that she had worn one of his bright red stickers (TURN ON TO JESUS) and "never had a better night!"[7] Sexual habits were the most difficult to change during this time. Some on university campuses, which were depreciatory of Jesus people, found it easy to shout "Jesus loves you!" and "Praise the Lord!" because it gave license to do whatever else they pleased. Organized campus groups suffered greatly and lost a generation of students in the process.[8]

Finally, those who reflected about what the revolution gave showed optimism, offered cautions, and made predictions about the Jesus Movement. Each response had validity.

Kenneth Chaffin, at this time the Baptist HMB's evangelism director, was amazed how these youths were reminding religious people once again of the doctrine of the Holy Spirit. The recovery of this doctrine emphasized that Christians bear witness in the power of the Holy Spirit, leaving the results to God.

This takes evangelism out of the selling category and puts it in the sharing one.

William Hendricks, then professor at Southwestern Baptist seminary, added that it was inevitable that secular people who are threatened by the rash of modern technology would seek emotional release. Worship needs an emotional expression for some types of individuals. The time had come for these young people, bombarded with drugs, free-style sex, and other so-called "freedom releases," to realize these activities did not give them meaning for the long haul of life. The "freedom releases" did not deliver; therefore, they turned to one man—Jesus. Theron Price of Furman University had predicted "the rise of an unrestrained religious enthusiasm to make up for the vacuum secularism [it] had created." He was a prophet.

So dramatic were the lifestyle changes in these young people that they were accused of being on drugs or alcohol. Frequent Bible readers will immediately think of Pentecost and the second chapter of Acts. Peter raised his voice and said, "Indeed, these are not drunk, as you suppose, for it is only nine o'clock in the morning. No, this is what was spoken through the prophet Joel: 'In the last days it will be, God declares, that I will pour out my Spirit upon all flesh, and your sons and daughters shall prophesy, and your young men will see visions . . .'" (Acts 2:15–17, NRSV). It may not have been the last days of the Lord, but it was the last days for these young people to find hope.

Other religious people, pastors in particular, raised cautionary flags for both the Jesus people and the church. James Monroe, a church pastor at Fort Walton Beach, Florida, cautioned the following:

> One could become attracted to the movement and not to Jesus, to enjoy the sensations and never know Jesus.

> One could make a superficial attachment to Jesus out of curiosity or personal need, like most of the 5,000 Jesus fed who were satisfied with bread but never ate the bread of life.

> One could see total involvement of growing spiritually, of finding a place of fellowship and a place of service, but being blind to the larger implications of one's faith as applied to racism, poverty, war, and pollution.

Monroe also found dangers for the church: a temptation to dismiss the movement as a fad failing to see in it the involvement of the Holy Spirit, a continuation of the hypocrisy that caused many young people to lose respect for the churches, an aloofness that failed to open hearts and doors to alienated youth.[9]

Walker Knight in the last chapter of his compilation, *Jesus People Come Alive,* is the one who became the accurate, almost uncanny, predictor of this movement. Knight foresaw the peaking of the Jesus Movement as 1972. Bull's-eye! The news quality of the movement passed. All people saw after 1972 was the residue in splinter groups, and soon to be gone were the potential and struggling churches that might have come from it.

The most serious problem came at the point of theology. There were little apologetics for roots to form to solidify the Jesus Movement. Every movement is time structured and this one was particularly short-lived because the participants were not taught the basics of the faith.

As the early 1970s continued, other ideas became more important than just finding a correction to the sixties. Someone wryly suggested that God can hit a strong lick with a crooked stick. That statement may be as good a summary as any for the Jesus Revolution.

The "New" Student in Transition

One should not assume *everything* in the sixties was wrong, that all students were total "protesters," or that the Christian message was passé. Early the next decade, student life began to change from one lifestyle to another.

The problem, as always, is how to vividly describe health in a better way than sickness or good in a more valid fashion than evil. No doubt, the "old" student had passed. These "new" students had too much knowledge to accept their elders' blind faith. They were too idealistic to see the "faith of the fathers" and "answers to prayer" in color televisions, split-level housing, and multimillion-dollar church buildings.

A great segment of the student population in this era knew where they were going. They were not in the rhythm of the regular chaos of the times. The news media gave this group little notice; they were not bizarre or sensational enough.

Professor Garff Wilson of the University of California at Berkeley wrote in 1967 about the majority of students on his campus. At that time his view was a minority one:

> In December, 773 people were arrested in the Sproul Hall sit-in. In that same semester 3,549 undergrads made the honor roll with a B average or better. You read that hundreds of dollars were raised to bail out sit-in students; in the same year $9,602 were raised by students for Cal Camp's under-privileged children and staffed by 50 volunteer students. You read that 4 students were arrested in the so-called 'dirty word' demonstration. In the same year 262 students spent 20,000 hours tutoring in Berkeley public schools. You read that mobs marched in parades protesting the Vietnam war. Did you know there are now serving in the peace corps 560 Cal students and 1,000 additional have volunteered? You read last March that 800 students walked out of Greek theater protesting Ambassador Goldberg, but did you read that 12,000 remained and gave him a standing ovation?[10]

Also, some publications, notably the *National Observer*, were reporting the fragmentation of such groups as the Students for a Democratic Society, questioning whether minority student group tactics were honorable and noting the slow demise of the Haight-Ashbury section of San Francisco. Some publicity was given to a majority student organization at Fresno State, who by wearing blue arm bands were saying, "Leave us alone. We want an education."

Among Baptists there were evidences that recognition needed to be given to the Christian student of the 1960s. In the October 1968 "Letters to the Editor" section of *Home Missions*, Walker Knight pointed out that though nine hundred summer missionaries were working under the auspices of the board, one hundred more could have been employed if funds had been available.

Baptist Press wrote of the final electrifying night during the 1968 Baptist Student Conference at Glorieta. In a student-led meeting, student speakers expressed concern for a needy world. At the conclusion of the service, one of the students shocked the conference by saying, "As an act of worship, I take my coat and leave it at the altar." After a pregnant silence, two to three hundred students filed down the aisles leaving "acts of worship"—mainly clothing. The poor of New Mexico benefited on a horizontal level from that which had been offered on a vertical relationship between young people and their God. These were evidences through secular and denominational presses of the "new" student in transition to the eighth decade of the twentieth century.

The haunting question arose, however, whether campus ministry and local church leadership would fill this transitional period with a meaningful ministry to meaningful students. Christian leaders—academic and church—were challenged to find new ways to interpret age-old verities (as "geared to the times, but anchored in the rock"). This era's student needed to be shown anew the possibility, the validity, and the adventure of Christian mission.

As terrible as the year had been, the redeeming event was the Apollo 8 Moon Mission in late December 1968. The same words for Christian reclamation—possibility, validity, adventure—must have been used over and over in preparing for and completing this mission. The language for the whole world to hear that Christmas Eve night was not scientific. It was the language of the Bible: "And God created the earth and it was good." The scientists understood the wonderful revelation given by God. They paid homage even as had the wise men of old before Bethlehem's babe.

At the end of the sensuous sixties and the beginnings of the self-centered seventies Christian validity, possibility, and adventure were to be recaptured in Christian thought on the campuses of academe. In their recapturing, the language had to be twentieth century parlance with biblical interpretation that would read like tomorrow's headlines if students were to be reclaimed for the faith.[11]

CONCLUSION: FROM DENOMINATIONAL CONSERVATION
TO RECLAMATION

By 1968 over one-half of the population of this nation was twenty-six years of age or younger. These youth had lived in prosperity, and most knew little of the

Great Depression, World War II, the Holocaust, or other historical crises. The years of their lives had been ones of unprecedented opportunity—education for the masses, technological marvels, and a knowledge explosion that would double every future decade. The times also had brought many strange ideas and alien philosophies.

Campus religious workers were confronted with what sociologists had chosen to call the "new" student. Their ways and thoughts were new in every respect. Christian faith and church faced its share of new thinking. Albert McClellan, program secretary for Southern Baptists' Executive Committee, had characterized these youth as "emerging young men." At least by this nomenclature, the gender issue was in the future.

These "emerging young men" had created gaps not only between the generations but also between themselves and the God of Abraham, Isaac, and Jacob. They had become self-reliant (almost self-centered) because of the knowledge explosion; they were alert that the culture was no longer rural oriented but urban centered. They questioned everything—idealism, morals, authority—and felt little obligation to anyone. The institutionalized church had failed them; yet, with wistful longing, they yearned for the church of the living God. In the 1990s this idea evolved to a sense of abandonment.

The new student was thought to have come from a church-related environment, but facts proved quite the contrary. Several state Baptist student departments during this time conducted surveys among Baptist freshmen to ascertain their church activities at home. The survey revealed that more than one-half had not attended a worship service or any other church activity during the previous seventeen months. In addition, students in their first year of higher education had a tendency to omit church from their activities for the first time. (Leslie Weatherhead, the great British preacher, once commented, "Young academicians never are sure whether they worship their God, or their mothers' [God], as when they are deciding whether or not to get out of bed on the first Sunday at the university and go to worship.") Student leaders confirmed what they feared— the new students did not come to college with church as a vital part of their lives.

Because of this astonishing revelation, new thought had to be given to what conservation for Baptists meant and what new role student religious work would devise. A new word—*reclamation*—became a focal point in student religious programs. BSU could no longer see its task only as conservation but had to begin a broader process of reclamation.

After all, this was just another need that student leadership saw they had to meet. This ministry was not a separate entity from local church programs. Those in leadership roles voiced no intention of isolating students from local church programs. Church isolation, as seen in other denominational, interdenominational, and nondenominational philosophies, had taught Baptist student leaders the ineffectiveness of such programs. Church should have been a vital part of every life in the academic community. Church met through the weekday ministry of BSU programs across the land; conversely, BSU met at church gatherings where students were present.

The ministry on campus developed new approaches and a new vocabulary—reclamation and church-relatedness. New national and world concepts could not be taught with the old student religious program terminology. The task by the end of the 1960s was to take New Testament truths and make these age-old verities clear and relevant to these students' minds. Because God's truth is relevant for every age, now it was time to articulate the Christian faith to a secular age.

If the student of the 1960s found any relevance in service, she/he found it in governmental programs—the Peace Corps, for instance. At this period in time, it was incumbent upon someone to teach a lesson about the results of faith. Christian mission through the ages, and student missions in recent history, have blazed paths for service to humanity's need. The definitive difference was, when God through Christ comes into both the heart and mind of nonbelievers or nominal believers, the spiritual dimension shows its imperativeness. The Christian saw others as persons who are fellow servants of God, whereas societal service saw only people in less fortunate circumstances. Ministry to students, at this time, had to show the difference between computerized service and Christian service.

The concept of BSU as a conservation agent needed reassessing. There was too much information that showed the late 1960s and early 1970s were the times to reclaim students for the church. The organization was no longer seen as church centered, but a new concept of church-relatedness was recognized by both BSU and local Baptist churches.

The times had changed!

The Director of Student Ministries as Professional
(A Lifelong Vocation)

Paradoxically, the role of the Baptist director of student ministries was developing professionally into a career vocation in the midst of the turmoil of two decades, 1957–1972. The "stepping-stone" time had passed.

In 1970 major changes were being made in the Sunday School Board's student department. Charles M. Roselle was elected secretary; Edward S. Rollins was elected manager of the department. There were now 267 full-time local directors, and a total of 516 local student workers, counting part-time and volunteer ones. There were 206 Baptist student centers across the land. The department's name was changed to National Student Ministry (NSM).[1]

This was the time and place for local Baptist student workers to consider a new terminology: *campus minister.* Other denominations had been calling their campus personnel by that title for a number of years. But, unfortunately, there were leaders in various state conventions who equated the term campus minister with those communions who had joined together for ecumenical work. Also, these state leaders wrongly assumed that this title meant very little—if any—programming. The term *Baptist campus minister* did not become prevalent until the early 1980s. More than likely, the title's first beginning was in newer territory areas of SBC.

In the early 1970s, feeble efforts were being made to form an association for local BSU directors similar to the state student directors. This was another effort to professionalize the work. As the state directors faced objections to their formation, so did the local ones—this time from a few state directors. However, almost the same reasons for this group to be formed were the ones the state organization had expressed in 1959. Various meetings, usually called by the state headquarters, were not meeting their particular needs.

In 1977 the Association of Southern Baptist Campus Ministers was formed. The purposes were to provide a forum to discuss problems as local workers, to invite speakers who were academic and religious experts, and to start a publication called the *Campus Minister.* This group annually awards the Campus Minister of the Year to one or more individuals for their achievements. Members of this organization recently celebrated their twentieth anniversary.

The solidifying efforts on the national level had a trickle-down effect on the rest of student work. More and more local personnel felt professional in their vocation. A title—campus minister—raised their place in academia.

Another major factor developed in the latter 1950s. The philosophy of *in loco parentis* was ending on university campuses. Universities announced that they would no longer be responsible for students as surrogate parents. That meant no longer were Baptist directors of campus ministries required to "student-sit" for every activity that BSU engaged. As leaders grew older, as family responsibilities developed, it was beginning to wear and tear on them to spend midnight hours looking after students in their charge. No longer having this duty allowed campus religious leaders to mature in years while continuing in their work. Maturity also brought out the best qualities of leadership. This ending of the role of campus officials serving in lieu of parents could not have come at a more fortuitous time. "Student-sitters," another unfortunate connotation of Baptist student workers, disappeared.

THE CHANGING ROLE OF THE CONVENTIONWIDE DEPARTMENT

G. Kearnie Keegan died of a heart attack September 13, 1960, while traveling to Hawaii to dedicate a BSU center on the Big Island. David K. Alexander was elected secretary of the Sunday School Board Student Department in July 1961.

Alexander's primary task was to finish the work on the stated philosophy of Southern Baptist student work and interpret it not only for campus constituency but also for Baptists as a whole. This task was important. For the first time since the work's inception, everyone felt involved in an enterprise that was academically valid. The faith not only had an emotional quality but also an intellectual one. Directors of student ministries now felt on the same plane as other adults in academe and could contemplate their work as a lifelong vocation.

It was on Alexander's "watch" that the agreement among different agencies was worked out—primarily HMB—to employ student workers at the service academies. The year was 1966. At the same time, the Conventionwide Student Department provided appropriations to employ directors of student ministries in new convention areas. It was not until 1966 that the campus ministries program, passed in 1962 by the state BSU directors, received approval by the convention.

Alexander spent his years reinterpreting a new program that was now national in scope. When he accepted a position at Vanderbilt University, Charles M. Roselle, state student director of Tennessee, was elected as his successor in 1970. Roselle was the first person elected to this office who had been both a local and a state BSU director.

Roselle's preparation allowed him to take this work through the "response" stage of Baptist student ministry. *Response* meant implementing the stated program on a national level. Also, the work included churches and every other agency of this denomination to reach students for Christ. For the first time, student ministry was emphasized in various places other than campus entities.

The new director of NSM launched the second fifty years of Baptist campus ministry with the hope it would be more than what the "first fantastic fifty" years had been. The target was a BSU on every campus nationwide and every church in the convention to consider itself a "college church."

To honor the fiftieth anniversary of BSU in 1972, the *Quarterly Review* gave its whole issue to the program. This publication was for the purpose of showing progress among Baptists. To emphasize the plan of church involvement, Roselle challenged everyone through the anniversary issue:

> Churches must minister to students. This begins with pre-college preparation and continues through the college years. The student may still be at home or he may be temporarily in the territory of a "college church." It has been repeated often, but is still true that "every church is a college church." Location speaks only to quantity. Every church has a responsibility to provide a student ministry. No matter the form, location, or sponsoring body of student ministry, it should be for Christ and in behalf of, related to, and supported by the churches.

> We have moved from a history of care for the Baptist student who is away from home at college to ministries to all students everywhere. We are turning a corner into a great new era challenged by new territories and new methods of ministry.[2]

Student ministries in SBC may have come full circle in fifty years. From the initial principle of being a program to conserve students for a denomination, it was now the water that surrounded every sponge of convention life—institution, agency, and church. It seemed to be Roselle's conviction that a determined response would be forthcoming from every segment of convention life. His observation that college students were being ministered to by many churches and agencies was true. This was not much different than in the early Leavell years. It was more sophisticated and complicated. His philosophy was simple yet profound.

Paraphrased, he was saying, "I'm in favor of everyone doing student work." On the surface his trying to get his goals accomplished through the "machinery" of SBC's organization may have seemed as if the student was being forgotten. However, he came back to first base. He said during his inaugural days, "Like all others, students are potentially church members, but more so they are the main leadership potential for the denomination's institutional and mission enterprises."

Roselle laid claim that the progress of Bold Mission Thrust—the ambitious mission program of the denomination culminating in the year 2000—would come through Baptist Student Unions. He coined the phrase to describe the past—Fifty Fantastic Years. The next half-century would still have the golden hue of the past, but would contain a Christian commitment to the *whole* academician instead of just the *soul* academician. There would be many twists and turns in the future that no one, at this time, thought possible.

The Rise of a New Vocation

Roselle, more than likely, did not realize that his saying he was in favor of everybody doing student work would give rise to a new vocation, minister to students in local collegiate churches. This new relationship between campus and church came about when students became more mobile, when more worked, and when more decided to live off campus. Also, the age of students was gradually increasing and more were married, or at least financially independent. All these factors demanded choices about how time was to be allotted. Frequently, students had to choose between church and BSU. Historically, mature directors of BSU always said, "If you have to choose between BSU and church, choose church."

In the early days of this new vocation, people chosen for these positions may have been youth ministers on church staffs. They lacked training to deal with the theological problems prominent in academe. Very few were oriented toward Bible studies geared to the thoughts of collegians. Student programs in local churches were more or less social in nature and fellowship groups. The initial programs involved the collegians who remained in their home churches. These early church student ministers did not have long tenure. This reminded everyone of the short tenures of early BSU secretaries.

In the usual evolution of time, seminaries began to realize another potential for reaching students. Courses were offered with only church students in mind. Also, these church groups received invitations to their respective state BSU conventions and retreats. Invitations were extended to Conventionwide meetings at the national assemblies. The Sunday School Board NSM now provides "experts" to lead seminars and discussion groups for church ministers to students. All of this was not accomplished without some soul-searching about the distinct roles of the director of student ministries and the church minister to students. There was the possibility of conflict between the two, but after a decade the church student ministers were equally trained.

Monthly meetings were scheduled, usually at BSU centers, for these two groups to discuss mutual strategies for reaching students for Christ. An example of recent programs at churches is in the First Baptist Church of Tallahassee. A look at what this particular church student minister is doing will reveal that BSU had moved across the street! Or is it a new way of conserving students for the church and denomination? Clint Purvis, minister to college students there, provides worship, counseling, social activities, Bible studies, and food—spiritual and phys-ical—to between 750 and 1000 Florida State, Florida A & M, and Tallahassee Community College students each week. Purvis observed, "They don't want friv-olity. They don't want to (just) be fed and entertained. What they want from their church is meaningful, in-depth Bible study and worship."[3]

The prevailing winds were ones of change. The fixed was becoming flexible. Theology was moving from personal experience to social action. Ethics were moving from codified conduct to situational behavior with everyone trying to find a balance between the two. Ecclesiology was moving from "the keepers of the key" to challenging the establishment of vested interests and then to striving for communities of caring believers. There was a confusion of tongues because of the acceleration of pluralism seen in modern culture, social endeavors, and religious life. There were jungles without trees—technology was proliferating life. Home sweet home was the site of domestic dislocation and the multiplication of family configurations. Better was becoming less because of the increasing demand of specialization, and, consequently, the humanities declined.

PROFILE OF A DIRECTOR OF STUDENT MINISTRIES AS PROFESSIONAL

What kind of person was willing to face the realities of the day? As the vocation of Baptist directors of student ministries was becoming more professional, how should his or her profile develop?

A Person for All Seasons

Is a campus minister a generalist or a "marginal person?" Perhaps both. He/she is an orchestrator.

A generalist is one who can answer, or knows where to find the answer, to the most inquisitive student's theological dilemmas. If the air-conditioning system is broken, she/he knows how to fix it. A sports-minded student wants to know baseball's Jackie Robinson's lifetime batting average—he asks his BSU director. That his religious leader has a nodding acquaintance with every academic discipline is a given in most students' minds. The whole university and the church community think Baptist student workers, somewhere along the way, received a CPA; therefore, they should be excellent administrators.

Yet this person is increasingly a "marginal" one—the one in the middle. She/he is the link between the community of learning and the community of faith. This, then, is the most creative position of all. Directors of student ministries stand with one foot in each camp, belonging to neither yet speaking to and for both. This person of all seasons is an orchestrator.

Bridge over Troubled Waters

By the middle 1970s, the second generation of BSU directors became middle-aged. They began to dream that this vocation would be their lifelong one.

Troubled waters demanded bridges—thus a second attribute needed polishing. Baptist student leaders became reconcilers. Not only was one foot in academe and the other in church, but also they saw two camps being formed within their own constituency of students.

Those young people who were products of the social actions of the soaring sixties were still around. On the horizon was the "me generation." This new group also was reflecting the conservatism of their nation. When "the controversy" reared its head in SBC, the "me generation" was ripe to become a part of fundamentalism.

Here the current campus ministers found themselves acting to reconcile the two groups.

However, reconciliation is a major theological trait; therefore, reconciliation should be in the profile of Christian leaders. This trait's main form is between person and God, plus between person and person. To build bridges over troubled waters one must be a reconciler.

Ambassador of the Unobservable Kingdom

Students of the Bible could claim the teachings of Jesus ultimately concerned the kingdom of God—that which was unobservable. In profiling a good campus minister one could call him or her a practical idealist—oxymoronic as that sounds. The leader of students deals every day with practical ways to convey an idealist message. The question is always: How is your daily living moving you toward being "perfect as your Father in heaven is perfect"? There is scholarly evidence that the word *mature* is more correct than the word *perfect*. None has achieved Christian perfection.

Students come in all shades and varieties of the Christian experience. A good campus minister takes them where they are, then patiently provides the tension at the place they need maturing. Finding Christ for the first time does not mean Christian maturity arrives simultaneously. Some freshmen are more mature in Christ than their senior counterparts.

This is the basis of being practical. This does not undercut the idealism of the unobservable kingdom. Good Baptist campus leaders will add *practical idealist* to their profile.

Every Person Matters

Here is the watershed that determines love for students. A successful and prominent Southern Baptist served as a campus student worker for a short time. Upon accepting a new position outside campus ministry, he reportedly said, "BSU could have been wonderful if it weren't for the students."

Yes, they come as invaders to solve all ills, as tourists to take only what they desire, usually food and fellowship, and as refugees who have fallen through cracks of other campus life. A good director of student ministries will be determined to turn them into pilgrims following the Galilean. If every person matters, every person needs affirming.

Affirmers are patient, trained counselors; affirmers interpret the positiveness of the good news; affirmers are those who model and equip themselves so that they can call the saints to ministry.

It is difficult to affirm everyone. There may be occurrences when affirmation is *not* the Christian answer to a student's actions or thought. The affirming process comes in the tension of the faith. It takes courage for a leader to take this tack. Someone once said, "Friends are the only people who have the right to hurt you."

That is correct. A good campus minister will know and risk that the statement is true. Persons matter to those who add to their profile *affirmer.*

The Image of God

It is a lot easier to act like God than it is to be human. Whatever one thinks of the Adam and Eve story, something is sure. After they left the garden, responsibility began concerning what it meant to be human. Innocence was lost.

A positive profile for campus ministers is their humanity. The Christian imperative surrounds one's maturing humanity. The model, colloquially, is "what you see is what you get!" in times of success and in times of battle. Perhaps the greatest detriment to students seeing the humanity of their leader is his or her use of "God language." The phrase "God is leading me to . . . " may be the greatest cover-up religious leaders use in hiding their humanity.

Their example should be Jesus of Nazareth. In his public ministry the people of Palestine saw what they got. A human was the Messiah! Paul wrote to the Ephesians, "He has abolished the law with its commandments and ordinances, that he might create in himself one new humanity . . ." (Eph. 2:15, NRSV).

Managing a Household Well

There may be many changes that have come about in campus ministry, but one characteristic needed by positive-living campus ministers has never changed. Their families should exemplify the Christian model. In a day of dysfunctional homes, here may be an island of pleasure that calms the fears of young people reading frightening statistics of American family life.

If the love of God should be shown anywhere, it is at home. What better place for it to shine for students? The profile of *lover of family* tends to make everything more believable in a BSU leader. To see love of family makes the work of the change agent easier elsewhere.

Priest and Prophet

Southern Baptists directors of student ministries in the past did not do many priestly functions, that is—as those functions are generally understood—preach, baptize, or preside at communion. However, they are priests if other connotations are discovered—maybe, rediscovered.

Historically, it did not take the second generation of Southern Baptist student workers long to discover they had the wrong type of seminary training. Most of them had higher degrees in religious education. The questions students asked were not how to build Sunday Schools or Training Unions. They wanted to know about who God is, and they wanted somebody to be able to enlighten them about the Word of God.

New leaders soon realized they had priestly functions in their job description. Proclaiming the faith did not mean standing behind "the sacred desk" only. It meant wise counsel day after day to questioning pilgrims as to what the Word means about this or that. Students accepted this type of priestly function of supporting inquiry in a variety of faith options. These faith options give foundations to responsible social issues.

More student leaders felt the need of ordination; more became voracious readers in theology; more became literate in the details of biblical knowledge. These priestly functions allowed them, at least, to act more authoritatively. They began serving as preaching interims and performing marriages for their constituents in gown and town.

The role of prophet wasn't new to this profession. They realized that, biblically speaking, prophecy was more *forthtelling* than *foretelling*. Workers with Baptist students have been doing this from the inception of the vocation. That is what attracted the first BSU secretaries; they stretched the parameters of the faith as far as the church would allow. The social issues of the day—their day—were their concern. The issues of civil and other rights and war were and are the way everyone should extend the gospel.

In this effort campus ministers should encourage faculty, students, and university administrators to participate and lead in local churches. This brings congregants knowledge of theological, ethical, and social developments that academics learn in the halls of ivy.

In the role of priests and prophets, BSU student leaders become facilitators. They teach basic biblical principles and train and call out the "saints" for the work of ministry. Today's leaders of Baptist students are lacking if their profile does not contain the description of priest and prophet.

No Lovelier Spot in the Dale

Lastly, but not completely, a BSU leader's profile should contain the noun *churchperson*. This profile has been modeled historically and magnificently.

Unfortunately, the day has come when denominational lines are no longer recognizable as one passes the Lord's sanctuaries in cities across America. It would seem the campus ministers would rejoice at the ecumenicity, but that is not what has happened. The disappearance of the word *Baptist* represents a loss of its meaning; in fact, the disappearance is to cover embarrassment of a denomination gone awry.

J. D. Grey, a giant among Southern Baptists and for decades pastor of the First Baptist Church in New Orleans, once voiced this concern:

> We need to have conviction about the principles that have made us what we are as Baptist people. For if we do not have conviction, then we will have a spineless generation, we will have an *anemic denomination* [italics mine], an insipid church, and members who are lacking in character, stamina, and enthusiasm.[4]

For a good director of Baptist student ministries, being a churchperson today means she/he is in the business of restoration. Students are "worshiping" at altars placed in front of televisions to listen to the "black" and "white" values of the faith as proclaimed by televangelists and pastors of super churches across the land. The battle is between confessions and creeds.

Historically, confessions were by those who said, "This we believe and you can't stop us from saying it." Hopefully, Baptists were saying, "Use the plumb line to see how close our confession is to the teaching of the New Covenant." Creeds, as has been seen the last decade and one-half, say, "This you must believe; shape up or ship out." A majority of students have shipped out. Someone remarked, "They are 'high' on God, 'low' on church, and its influence is waning daily."

So what is a campus minister to do? Flee the church in the dell or the concrete jungle? No! As church member, here again is a place for prophets. These folk stretched the parameters of the faith in the past. Campus leaders are called again to risk themselves for the future of God's church. If the denomination called Baptist is worthy, campus leaders should proclaim their rich doctrines that admittedly have never been clear-cut but are proclaimed from the element of faith.

Restoring the church may take building anew, a freshness of the morning breeze, an imagination that leaves everyone dizzy from excitement, and replenishment in different modes. Both the words *church* and *Baptist* are precious ones—though tarnished in the 1990s. What better compliment can a campus minister hear than "What a great churchperson!" Great churchpersons provide tension against the *status quo*.

A Profile Conclusion

Others would add to this profile. Perhaps *theologian* should be appended, for one has to speak and teach Christian and Baptist doctrine, comparative religion, and ecclesiology. Creators of public policy are needed for "town and gown" if the Christian faith is understood in the context of everyday activity. Civic activity gives opportunity to be heard on the issues that face municipalities—the issues of the homeless and hungry are ever present. Administrators are needed so the biblical term *stewardship* will be manifested. Unfortunately, most spiritual connoisseurs seem to feel they are above the mundane tasks concerning material things. They need to be reminded that *administrator* has *ministry* at its center. Patrons of the arts are needed, for few see religious vocational workers as those who are well-versed in classical music, theatre, and other art endeavors as they should be.

The second generation of Baptist campus leaders, for the most part, provided excellent examples of this cumulative profile. They were also mostly in their fifth decade of life and were beginning to think of the possibility of retiring in another decade or two from their present vocation. The vocation, the program, and the leaders matured simultaneously. Philosophical depth was apparent in the work.

No longer were church people wondering when young campus leaders were going to leave their "cheerleading" or "spiritual coaches" jobs.

JOINING THE CORPORATION

Throughout this writing the allusion has been made to campus people as those outside the general leadership of Southern Baptist life. Campus ministry existed for a long time in the shadows. The reasons were many: short tenures and little educational opportunities for this group, but mainly there was an unhealthy suspicion among the general populace of Baptists that education made a person less spiritual.

Upon becoming accepted, someone decided campus ministers should become part of the rest of the leaders. That meant no more lonely vigils in the halls of ivory. More caution was needed in speaking to issues. Now they represented the whole state convention. One character said, "My stationery should read 'Associate State BSU Director.' I felt like I had sold my soul to the company store."

This "lonely crowd" was now required to attend all staff meetings at the state level. What affected one staff person affected all. One positive note was on the financial scale. Everyone was on the same salary level, and that benefited most campus people. State-level meetings and higher salaries reflected acceptance and arrival for members of campus ministry; it also meant that they became part of the vicissitudes of denominational life.

CONCLUSION

All the expansion and success in BSU was not accomplished in the decade of the 1970s. Actually, the foundation began earlier. Historians should examine closely the impact of Atlanta's HMB during this time. What was about to happen would tremendously affect student programs across the convention. With leadership's encouragement, HMB was about to open windows of fresh breezes turning into strong winds of mission endeavor.

In 1959 four individuals who came to the board almost simultaneously became catalysts for change: They were Arthur Rutledge, the new executive director; Glendon McCullough, director of an expanded personnel department; Emmanuel McCall, director of relations to black pastors and churches; and Walker L. Knight, editor of *Home Missions* magazine. They would set the mission course of Southern Baptists from that time through the seventies. Simply stated, these men charted new paths and, at that time, made HMB the Southern Baptist agency that established new parameters of the faith.

During the 1960s the Special Ministries Department of this agency inaugurated new short-term programs, primarily for students. Warren Woolf was the director and soon asked R. Donald Hammonds to join him as associate in summer missions. Both of these came from local campus ministry positions. Hammonds later assumed Woolf's position and ultimately became the acting vice president of the Ministries Section of the board.

The work of this department was as responsible for the huge numbers of volunteers, whose work culminated in more professions of faith per person, as any other entity at the board. In 1992 a Mission Section review by Michael Robertson, director of Short-Term Volunteer Department, showed that this group had supervised 60,284 volunteers and reported 51,796 professions of faith. The professions of faith were 47 percent of HMB's total.

In the 1970s BSU programming had become a tremendous Conventionwide success. Thousands of students were reached each year for Christ. Conventionwide agencies were looking more and more to students as they expanded summer missions, US-2, and Journeyman programs.

Short-term programs such as SPOTS helped church construction in newer territory areas, provided beach ministries during spring breaks, and ministered at ski resorts during Christmas and winter school breaks. (There seems to be nothing out there in the land but that a mission project can help.)

Campus ministries won the hearts of knowledgeable Southern Baptists in the 1970s. After inception Baptist campus ministry finally became accepted as an integral part of Southern Baptist life. It was a far cry from the time BSU veterans knew everyone in their work by name; in the mid-seventies Baptist directors of student ministries numbered between 750 and 900.

BSU had withstood the fiery flames of disrespect, ridicule, doubt, and, most of all, suspicion. From this crucible had come a diamond—fresh, sparkling, and cut according to the deepest needs of Southern Baptists' collegians, a diamond whose gleam carried around the globe the missionary message "Go ye and make disciples of all persons." Students could say with the apostle Paul, "I am not ashamed of the gospel; it the power of God for salvation to everyone who has faith . . ." (Rom. 1:16, NRSV).

Alas, there were two coal-colored clouds on the horizon of the late seventies. They would bring the storms of the aching eighties. The first—a thunderstorm— was the narcissism of a nation. The "me generation" ultimately infiltrated academe and trickled into Baptist Student Unions. The result was the carbuncle of conservatism. The second—a tornado—was the fallout from the controversy in SBC that began in 1979 and has continued. The BSU diamond's brightness was in danger of dimming.

Living in a Smaller Biosphere
(SBC's Campus Ministry at Crossroads)

Students of trends have the benefit of time for the general public to be rather comfortable with titles of past eras or decades. They also understand—although they continue to divide them—that new eras do not come in neat packages of ten years. Phrases tend to stick, however, such as the fitful fifties, the soaring sixties, the slovenly seventies, and the aching eighties.

The aching eighties may still be too recent for validation. Some trendsetters even see this period from 1980 to the present as a time of "living within the parentheses." There are no major trends, just a series of glitches on the radar. To paraphrase the pessimistic view of poet T. S. Eliot, "We won't go out with a bang, only a whimper; leaving a legacy of asphalt roads and a thousand lost golf balls."

Those who surround themselves with hope—even Christian hope—still may judge this time as one of living within the parentheses or a smaller biosphere. When will the courageous burst the seams of the biosphere? When will they heed again the admonition of the apostle Peter and "sanctify the Lord God . . . always to *give* an answer to every man that asketh you a reason for the hope that is in you . . ." (1 Pet. 3:15, KJV)? That hope demands radiant living on both the perpendicular and horizontal levels.

Southern Baptists have always lived in a contained theological and cultural biosphere. In the middle 1970s, students were developing a narcissism that became a well-defined biosphere of self-centeredness. Almost simultaneously, 1979 to be exact, SBC created a smaller theological biosphere that would exemplify "the controversy." The rhythm of regular chaos reigned, even up to the present. Both of these turning points—narcissistic students and the Conventionwide controversy—would change the character of student ministry of this denomination.

CROSSROADS ONE—LIBERALISM OR CONSERVATISM

Liberalism is a great word! It makes this nation great. Freedom comes out of this concept. Individuals can believe as they wish. Out of this root come the people called Baptists and—yes—other communions.

From the late 1970s, liberalism became a dirty word both politically and religiously. Students were caught in this new syndrome. The shift from liberal to moderate to conservative students perhaps reflected the absence of such incendiary issues as the Vietnam War. Correspondingly, the conservative impasse became prevalent as the nation moved in that direction with the beginning of the Reagan administration in 1980.

This apparent liberal decline seems surprising in view of the continuing strength of student attitudes on women's rights and the legalization of marijuana. Perhaps liberal positions by students had become so common that now they were labeled as merely *moderate*. By 1978—the usual scholarly birth date for the culture of narcissism—freshmen considered themselves middle-of-the-roaders, yet supported liberal positions on energy, pollution, and consumer protection. Women who viewed the Bible as the inerrant Word of God strangely refused to give up their maiden names at the advent of marriage.

The First Crossroads Result—Narcissism

Certainly, Christopher Lasch, because of his book *The Culture of Narcissism,* became the godfather of what was to be colloquially known as "me-ism." Others were worried as well. Ellen Goodman of the *Boston Globe* wrote a New Year's column in 1981:

> I was thinking of a real new year, the sort of year that comes awash in toasts, swaddled in hope. But 1981 has arrived middle-aged, rather wary and worried. There is a tightness around the edge of Americans this January, a tenseness in the national jaw line. People aren't eager to embrace 1981. They are braced for it. . . .

> The season is not ripe for negation, compromise and sharing. This is the year for authority, control and power. . . . Even theologians who deal with the mysteries of eternity, the complexity of the world, and the ethical dilemmas of human life are now told to go by The Book.[1]

David Nyhan in the Little Rock *Arkansas Gazette* a few weeks before President Reagan's second term election wrote a column titled "Why Young People Like Ronald Reagan":

> A generation [students] whose span of concentration runs to bumper stickers and album titles likes Reagan's one-liner approach to the world.

> The young are not fond of civil rights. All they know of affirmative action is that some black may get ahead of them on the list for medical school, or some Hispanic may get the mailman's job they've been angling for. The fact that

nearly 50 per cent of all black teenagers do not hold jobs is of little concern to white youths—they want theirs. . . .

The young have shelved the Depression. They do not realize that the Democratic Party—over the opposition of the Republicans—won them welfare and food stamps, unemployment and workmen's compensation, Social Security, Medicare, Medicaid. All the young know of food stamps is that the person ahead of them at the convenience store just bought six cans of Coke and some jelly doughnuts, and that's not right.

They know nothing of John Kennedy, whom Reagan contemptibly libeled, in a private letter to Nixon, as advocating policies similar to Marx's and Hitler's. The young shrug that off; it means nothing in their value system. They are selfish, and they have been poorly served by their elders, too many of whom lost their idealism, their commitment to equal rights, to paying for the less fortunate, to saying that squeezing the weak to benefit the strong is wrong.

They are a me-first generation under a me-first administration in a me-first world. *We all made them the way they are* [italics mine]. We deserve what they will give us: Me-Firstism.[2]

Maybe these writers, especially Nyhan, were a bit harsh, but in nearly all of the literature above, the sentiment was similar. Something in the 1980s was wrong, and that was affecting student religious groups. Christian student movements have always been on the sharpest edge of the faith. The Haystack Prayer meeting of 1806 led to a world mission movement; YMCA from the 1850s to the morning of the twentieth century brought Christ to every campus in the Northeast and South; students from Texas and Mississippi launched BSU; Baptist students of the late 1940s quickly involved themselves in summer missions of the Baptist HMB; in the 1950s Christian students helped crush the snake of segregation. That cutting edge no longer existed in the large numbers of the past. The students of the aching eighties (Christians included) were reflections of the conservatism of their parents, churches, and nation from which they were spawned.

Daniel Yankelovich was correct when, in his book *New Rules*, he illustrated changing values as a slight volcanic tremor *under* the earth that has caused great eruptions *on* the earth. Values had changed in the 1980s, both right and left, and the American public hadn't noticed.

John Naisbitt concluded in *Megatrends*:

We are *living in the time of parenthesis* [italics mine], the time between eras. It is as though we have bracketed off the present from the past and the future, for we are neither here nor there. We have not quite left behind the either/or

America of the past—centralized, industrialized, and economically self-contained. With one foot in the old world where we lived mostly in the Northeast, relied on institutional help, built hierarchies, and elected representatives, we approach problems with an eye toward the high-tech, short-term solutions.

But we have not embraced the future either. We have done the human thing: we are clinging to the known past in fear of the unknown future. . . . Those who are willing to handle the ambiguity of this in-between period and to anticipate the new era will be a quantum leap ahead of those who hold on to the past. The time of the parenthesis is a time of change and questioning.[3]

What did Southern Baptists and NSM leaders do in this time of living in the parenthesis? (One must not assume even in the present that everyone is still not living in the parenthesis.) What did they do with students who were not only narcissistic but also more cultural than Christian? Finally, how did students recover the abundant life in Christ? Or did they?

CROSSROADS TWO—NATIONAL STUDENT MINISTRIES: A TIME OF TRANSITION

The early 1980s was a time of transition for the NSM group at the Baptist Sunday School Board in Nashville. Charles Roselle retired in 1983. After a period of time, Charles Johnson, state campus ministry director of Missouri, was chosen to head the department. Johnson was a relatively unknown quantity to leaders of student ministries over SBC. These leaders were curious as to the direction he would lead the work.

In the coming years, Johnson and associates in NSM—who supposedly were the head of all Southern Baptist campus ministry—found themselves working in a tightly structured and rigid biosphere. This was a result of "the controversy." Also, living in the time of parenthesis caused a period of confusion for everyone trying to devise new programming for a new type of student. Then, too, a decision about the future major thrusts of NSM was imminent. Would the department continue to program for those in the "old and primarily Southern territory" or would they concentrate on the more national "newer convention territory"?

Last, there were those who wanted to turn local campus ministry into a more churchly direction. This was one of the results of churches hiring ministers to students. However, the most likely reason for the time was that students of the 1980s were not attending anyone's church.

The crossroads facing NSM were programming in light of "the controversy," concentrating on newer territory areas, and emphasizing the local church.

Programming for the 1980s Student

Everyone was so confused about what to do with narcissistic, conservative students that polls abounded. Counts ran the gamut from a survey at the Student Conference at Glorieta, New Mexico, in 1982, to Public Opinion Magazine's 1984 poll. The former had little actuarial value compared to the latter one. Interestingly enough, both polls showed a wide range of contradiction of value systems. For example in the Glorieta poll, 84 percent wanted a strong military defense, but out of the 369 responses, the same group contained 64 percent who were conscientious objectors. Almost everyone polled considered themselves "moderate" or "progressive," yet 90 percent were anti-ERA. The scarce majority of 51 percent in world-hunger efforts emphasized the lack of "playing out the faith" against personal piety. These were Baptist students NSM was having to program for in the coming years. What a task!

The same personal piety syndrome during these years was evident in the type of students who applied for summer missions and the US-2 programs at HMB. They were not always the best students on campus nor did as many apply as had been available in the 1960s. Some positions that needed filling in both programs were left vacant because HMB personnel refused to send those who lacked the spiritual qualifications that the work demanded.

A paper written for the Baptist Sunday School Board Research Department discovered that students possessed eight needs that required analyzation under the microscope of the Christian faith:[4]

> *Self-worth.* Conservative theology has always reminded Christians what worms they are. Lack of self-worth gives no emphasis to grace and love; therefore, it paralyzes the personality to consider the impact on social issues. Jesus said, "You should love your neighbor as *yourself.*" If one has poor self-concepts, he/she sees those same concepts in others. If one develops good self-concepts, he/she finds grace, love, and the abundant life in Jesus Christ in others.

> *Creative Doubt.* Robert M. Baird in an article in the *Journal of Religion and Health* suggested four arguments in defense of creative doubt:
>
> 1. Creative doubt is a means of constructively acknowledging human limitations.
> 2. Creative doubt can play a role in keeping one's fundamental beliefs from becoming dead dogmas.
> 3. Creative doubt recognizes most, if not all, language about God is symbolic. . . . It checks against idolatry.
> 4. Creative doubt involves challenging the value of the quest for certainty.[5]

Students who take Christianity seriously must realize that the one who never doubts the adequacy of symbols is worshipping his symbols. For Southern Baptists, church is the primary symbol; the Bible may be another. To worship symbols is to worship pointers to God; to worship something other than God is idolatry. Therefore, creative doubt may serve as a check against idolatry.

Identity. Ronald Brown, state student director in Maryland has written, "Identity means students need to know: what it means to be male and female (sexual identity); how to establish personhood separate from parents; [and] that 'I am,' with the belief that 'I' can cause change, make decisions, and be responsible."[6]

Fear of Failure Versus Hope and Success. Because students of the 1980s were so career oriented, their years in the university were more vocational than educational. This bred fear of failure, lack of hope, and a lack of understanding about what success meant in relation to the totality of life. For those involved in the Christian faith, these aspects were particularly damning.

These Christian students were insecure; they lost their sense of humor. They did not reflect the words of Jesus when he said in John 10:10 (RSV), "The thief comes only to steal . . . and destroy [fear of failure]; I came that they may have life and have it abundantly [hope and success]." Why should they not, in this present world, have been depressed and developed fears of failure when viewing the "News at Noon"? Terrorism, hunger, nuclear warfare, budget deficits, and student suicides had reached the national average; unemployment was rampant; housing costs were astronomical; and political leadership was almost nonexistent. Students needed to recall that Jesus said, "In the world ye have tribulation: but be of good cheer; I have overcome the world" (John 16:33b, KJV).

Temptation Versus the Cult of Confession. Temptations were very subtle in the lives of students in the 1980s. One can say their personal piety was about as pure as it had been for two decades. (Some would disagree with this, particularly in relation to sex.) However, there was also a subtlety in ridding themselves of temptation. This was by a formula: sin, confess, and then start over again. They loved to sin because they loved to confess. This phenomenon has recurred in student life during the middle 1990s under the guise of "revival."

Student temptations were more in the realm of succumbed *omission* than *commission.* They lacked joy, grace, sensitivity, and the sixth need—good interpersonal relationships. They prayed, confessed, read their Bibles, and let the rest of the world go to hell. Their Christian witness was what Jesus has done for *me* not what Jesus can do for *you*—religious narcissism.

Interpersonal Relationships. The primary need of this decade's students was a developmental one. They needed to learn how to give, receive, and communicate. Ferris Jordan, an educational psychologist teaching at New Orleans Baptist Seminary, gave the following ideas on improving the relationships of novice adults.

He stated that "giving measurements" is more than keeping distances from fellow students. Students must be willing to let other persons "in" and yet retain what they are. Can one enter another person's world and not "straighten them out?" Can a person learn to communicate acceptance? Can a person give in such a way that the encounter is one of pilgrimage?

The second method of improving relationships, according to Jordan, is by "receiving measurements," that is, letting another person know and love him or her. How can students let others help their potential and increase their respect?

Communication is more than "What's your name, your major; Where do you live?" This is at cliche level. Communication moves from clichés to report (just the facts, ma'am) to judgment (Why am I afraid to tell you who I am?) to healing and peak levels. Peak levels of communication are those that show active ways of accepting and listening. Students needed challenging during these days to develop interpersonal relationships.[7]

Intimacy. Students needed to know that they were heard, accepted, and cared about. They wanted their ideas taken seriously—their choices and decisions respected. They wanted to explore sexual feelings and drives—and how to get closer to another person *without* sex. They needed BSU and smaller groups who deeply believed in and cared about each other. They wanted to be close to, yet separate from, people in authority.[8]

Faith Development. The most intriguing book on faith development in the 1980s was James Fowler's *Stages of Faith.* His definition of faith development was "Faith is not dogma, it is a process and it must develop if we are to mature."[9]

When Fowler writes about faith and its development, he means a universal experience:

We all need to make sense of our lives. I began to understand that faith involves one's dynamic way of making meaning, and everyone engages in it. I also recognize that our culture strips away the power of faith by using the word as a static noun, rather than an active verb. One doesn't "have faith" or "lose faith." Faith continually grows or changes.[10]

These statements by James Fowler raised questions in the 1980s as to whether or not campus ministers were sensitive to where students were in their faith development. If ministers were not sensitive, they were answering questions no one was asking. Also, did these student leaders provide support to their constituency when they were trying to move through faith stages that provided Christian maturity?

People like Ircel Harrison, state student director of Tennessee, considered the value of "sponsorship" in spiritual formation/discipleship development. The sponsor was "a person or community [that] provides affirmation, encouragement, guidance, as models for another person's ongoing growth and development." The role of the sponsor was not only to support but also to confront, if necessary, and to challenge another to face difficult issues and self-deceptions. That would be a good description of the role of the campus minister and the community of faith on campus.[11]

CROSSROADS THREE—NSM'S RESPONSE: INWARD OVER OUTWARD

At the birth of the Baptists' student program, the logo (three links of intertwined chain with the words *student, campus,* and *church* written within) was developed that emphasized conservation of a denomination for the church. As the years went by, as students became more mobile, and as many churches became student churches, the logo lost its original meaning. In early days the church nearest campus was the student church.

During the 1970s NSM created a new logo, one with arrows devised circularly —white ones pointing inward representing the inward Christian journey, and black ones pointing outward representing the outward Christian journey. Since BSU was now more church related than church centered, the logo was to represent a balanced view. This led NSM to struggle with meeting students' needs through materials and services, which included relationships to churches, and to deal with the tension between being national in scope or continuing to program and emphasize student ministry mainly in old convention states. (Old convention states formed an inverted arc across the nation from D.C. to Maryland and south through New Mexico.)

The Materials and Services of NSM

John Naisbitt's words in the 1980s' *Megatrends* were correct: America was living in the parenthesis of time. With the advent of the computer technological world, soon to be the information highway, new trends seemed to be developing constantly. Therefore and no wonder, when anyone peruses the literature published by NSM, one word—*ambiguous*—comes to the forefront.

The symbol of national student work reflects the inward-outward Christian journey. Unfortunately, the majority of materials for this decade were dedicated to inner journeying—the cult of "me-ism." Only a minority of student work concerned social action. Piety, the inward life, overshadowed the demands of the outward journey of the faith. NSM was emphasizing one part of the logo to the detriment of the other.

If the 1982 report to SBC was given to NSM's new director as the basis for a different philosophy of student ministries, then one finds two interesting trends. First, this report equated conservative students to conservative churches as if this, in essence, was the beloved community. It said more about the kingdom of culture. Secondly, this report was an attempt to convince conservative churches that student ministry was very church centered.[12]

The fact was students in this time frame were not attending anyone's church in great numbers. Baptist Student Unions should not be blamed for this phenomenon; "church" for students had become the television screen on which Sabbath televangelists were exclaiming the virtues of the inner-Christian life.

Until this convention report, the question of student church attendance had not seriously risen. That brought about another issue, whether or not Baptist Student Unions were "para-church groups"—as was Campus Crusade for Christ. The total report raised questions Baptist people had not considered.

By 1997 state Baptist papers were reporting that SBC leaders were discussing the possibility of cooperation with Campus Crusade in youth evangelism. Also, reports surfacing in 1997 have been that the North American Mission Board will have a place for campus evangelism in the new organizational structure.

In the light of creating a smaller biosphere, a look at the materials of NSM is enlightening. Historically, although NSM is not a profitable enterprise, the materials had been written by the most capable people Southern Baptists had to offer, and they were excellent and relevant to the living of those days. Frank Stagg, Penrose St. Amant, Duke McCall, and Foy Valentine are only a few examples of the many outstanding writers and thinkers. The most outstanding writing was found in the *Baptist Student*, later called the *Student*. (The change of name was for the purpose of attracting a wider readership.) This monthly magazine presented a wide range of subjects about the Christian faith that pertains to students. The material was not only spiritual in content but it wrestled with the social issues of the day. The contents challenged students to activate the beloved community on earth. The kingdom of Christ is not of this world, but this world is the place where those who proclaim that kingdom have to live.

The willingness of the various editors through the years to challenge the *status quo* of the land was ongoing when Howard Bramlette became the editor. The times had changed. More and more the articles, and even writers, were being questioned about their theological "truth"—another effect brought by the developing fundamentalism of the convention. When Bramlette printed an article on the ordination of women, it proved to be the last straw. He was relieved of his position after a three-decade career in campus ministry.

Most of the 1980s' literature accentuated piety for students. Sunday School lessons were added to the *Student* to accentuate church. Numerous publications began to appear for discipleship groups. Some of these were *Share Seminar Material*, which were evangelistic in nature. *Masterlife* and *The Spiritual Journey Notebook* were to help develop students' maturity and their inward spiritual lives. There were suggested outreach sections in the latter book.

Almost nowhere was there anything that would help young people with the issues of love, courtship, and marriage; nuclear holocausts; a hungry world; career decisions; or everyday adolescent problems. Various campus ministers gave different answers as to what discipleship meant; they were confused as to purpose and questioned the huge amount of time spent by students in programs, particularly *Masterlife*. (*Baptist Today* published a cartoon of a Christian hovering over the victim in the Good Samaritan story saying, "I'll leave you a copy of the four spiritual laws, and if you need anything else, when I get back, I'll be certified to teach *Masterlife*.") These programs were developing *soul* people, not *whole* people.

One piece of material, *The Baptist Student Union Guidebook* has been, and still is, an excellent piece of organizational and planning literature. This book will fit any size or type of BSU. It is probably the most used material from the national office. Newer territory students have found it particularly useful, as will larger groups in the South.

CROSSROADS FOUR—NEW RELATIONSHIP WITH CHURCHES

One of the greatest changes in the transition from Roselle to Johnson in 1983 was the attempt to make the NSM program more church centered. The moot point now is whether the department succeeded. Through the years there had always been questions about the synthesis of BSU with local congregations. With the fundamentalists' wing becoming ever present and financial resources for campus ministry being questioned, the place of the church with students became, once again, paramount.

The Doctrine of Church

As far back as 1978, a theological perspective was attempted for BSU. The doctrine of church was a major part of that endeavor.[13] This doctrine was explored as BSU being church—a long source of tension.

A casual glance at the history of all student movements—not just the student program of Southern Baptists—reveal this tension as a continual one. Early twentieth century denominational student movements were founded for only two purposes: to save students for their denomination and to protect them from "corrosive acids of rationalism"—in other words, the university. For good or ill, these early times set the tone for such terms as "mission to the campus," "the arm of the church," and "the link to the church." Consequently, these terms created problems in the doctrine of church that remain to this present day.

As multichurch situations developed around campuses, it became obvious that campus ministry could not "deliver" students to a particular Baptist church. The "link" idea had heard the toll of death.

However, the theological problem was still on the scene. What was church? Did the word *church* connote place or purpose? What about the promise of Jesus when He declared, "For where two or three are gathered in my name, I am there among them" (Matt. 18:20, NRSV). Leo Armstrong, former pastor of First Baptist Church, Denton, Texas, was shepherd for a large group of two collegian communities. He said at a church-campus seminar, "Too long we have skirted the theological implications of BSU and the doctrine of the church. They could be both and the same. Baptist campus ministry is church; it is an organism with Christ at its helm. He who is the Way, Truth, and Reality comes to the academic community. Student movements' history shouts He has sanctified them."[14]

Carefully note that the articles *a* and *the* are not used. Leaders of student ministries have all been committed institutionally to the bride of Christ despite its many weaknesses. The church in New Testament epistles is, on the whole, a visible one with visible witnesses.

That is the reason Baptists have not recognized on-campus churches as viable. The witnesses of Christ must not gather at the place of many levels [the university] but at the place of no levels [the institutional church]. Witnesses for Jesus should not confine themselves to a one-age group but to a many-age group—from nursery to senility. This idea is a safeguard, if nothing else. It distinguishes the permanent mission of Christians from the transient mission of the university. It makes transition to church after university days almost painless. The theological problem of "place" over "purpose" solves itself easily when all seek Him who wants everyone in "town and gown" to know truth.

Pragmatically, church is Baptist campus ministry during the week; Baptist campus ministry meets in churches on Sundays—and at various other occasions. This is not two programs—it is one, a united effort to magnify Him who is the Christ.

Student work is a ministry to churches as well as a ministry to students. Therefore, campus ministers should become church ministers also. They should be the people with the most expertise in the ways of academe to help churches identify and develop their own unique ministry to collegians.

Raison d'être for Church Ministers to Students

Although the staff position of church minister was discussed elsewhere in this volume, there is reason to discuss the subject again from a different and troubling viewpoint. In the eyes of some very mature and long-tenured pastors, there were programs in the eighties' Baptist Student Unions that made them think campus ministries were veering from their historical roots. That, perhaps, was not true except that certain aspects of programming were going to extremes. Some program extremes that were occurring on Sundays caused students to stay away from the church. Also, mature pastoral leadership was concerned at the loss of Baptist history and doctrine. They felt BSU programming was omitting these vital parts of Baptist heritage.

Two other factors concerned these seasoned pastors about 1980s' students. Why did students tend to go to churches that had jazzy, emotional music? Why did they go to hear preachers who had little, if any, seminary training?

Robert Magee, senior pastor of Temple Baptist Church, Ruston, Louisiana, for more than twenty-five years, was questioned about why he intended to add a minister to students to the church staff. His reply was candid and revealing.[15] There was an undertone of trying desperately to get students back in the mainstream of Southern Baptist life. He began by showing frustration:

> I cannot understand why students can sit in classrooms with Ph.D.s during the week and then go hear an untrained minister on Sunday! However, that is the norm in our college community today. . . .
>
> Therefore, I sincerely hope that bringing a Minister to students to our church will do the following:
>
> 1. Reach more students for one church than BSU Directors can for all churches.
> 2. Commit himself to a consistent and stable atmosphere that will enable this segment of the church to grow.
> 3. Be *visible* on the campus and a *liaison* between the church and Baptist Student Union.
> 4. Develop a teaching community through Weekend Retreats that will enhance Bible Study programs to: 1) Recover Baptist doctrine; 2) Develop methods of interpretation which will include the *whole* Bible; 3) Develop self-worth from a Christian perspective; 4) Interpret the *whole* program of Southern Baptists; [and] 5) Move from pietism [Christian me-ism] to the totality of the faith.
> 5. Recover the great music traditions of the church.

Robert Magee was intimating that BSU students were spending too much time in such activities as singing groups. They were going to various places on Sundays for the purpose of raising funds for student summer missions. He was disturbed that this was happening more and more frequently—perhaps three out of four Sundays—though he supported Baptist students' involvement in missions.

Student ministry programs were being done. An employee of HMB reminded everyone that as a part of BSU programming each year thousands of students volunteered for mission projects. The interesting part was the different objectives of moderates and fundamentalists. Moderates did ministry as caring Christians to others who were hungry, homeless, or hurricane refugees with the hope of finding some nonchristians to introduce the Savior. Fundamentalists did ministry in order to save souls. Another member of the HMB staff told of an incident, which verifies the difference, during a mission activity after the devastating hurricane in Homestead, Florida.

A volunteer was weary after spending three or four hours serving food. He asked another person, who had a handful of salvation tracts, if he would relieve him for a while. The reply was, "I didn't come down here to serve food; I came to save souls." (If adults live in a tent-size biosphere, why should more be expected of young collegians?) However, Baptist Student Unions were majoring on inner-journey programs—such as long-term MasterLife activities—that demanded almost all of a student's limited time. Some pastors thought Baptist Student Unions were violating their historical purposes. When that happens, Baptist student organizations should beware. Charles Johnson's attempt at restoring church's place in campus ministry was a Herculean task and the right idea, but other encumbrances were taking precedent.

CROSSROADS FIVE—NEW CONVENTION WORK

There is much value in concentrating on newer territory areas of SBC. In these areas are the majority of megauniversities; consequently, here are huge numbers of students—a major portion of whom are nonchristian. For NSM to go in this direction would accomplish another goal. It would please the preeminent evangelistic emphasis of fundamentalists who were rapidly controlling the convention.

The aching eighties were just that —aching. One remembers what a character said in James Joyce's, *Ulysses,* "History can be a nightmare from which everyone is trying to wake." However, the work in new territory areas was the bright spot of the decade.

The joint mission of HMB's Special Ministries Department and NSM opened venues for student ministries in far-reaching places of the nation. Working through volunteers seemed to be the answer for areas that couldn't finance career campus ministers.

Innovative ideas and collegians who were willing to put on hold one or two years, or longer, their chosen careers dotted the Northeast, Midwest, and western regions. People like Robert Hartman from Nashville, and Michael Robertson, William Lee, Donald Hammonds, and more recently, Van Simmons from Atlanta combed the country enlisting these young people, fresh from college, who did not have the knowledge to know they couldn't do the job. They were like drops of rain in a vast dessert, but they were drops. They were young Abrahams and Sarahs who were going, they knew not where, and the whispering God was guiding them.

Countless academicians, outside the usual Southern Baptist realm, now were among the seekers and faithful.

Neither should one forget that the budgets of the Baptist Sunday School Board and HMB would have been very deficient for collegians if it had not been for the finances raised by members of Baptist Student Unions back home. To some extent this idea has been overlooked and could have resulted in a cessation of, particularly, summer missions' personnel and dollars. It was these BSU groups who not only provided the financial resources but also human ones. Not until 1996 did both of these boards see the need for a liaison person to work and encourage the older Baptist Student Unions in what they were contributing to the whole national program.

There may be reason now to question terminology used in their work. "New work" in "new territories" makes little sense anymore. Certain personnel and programs have been a part of these areas for a long time. State conventions, such as California, have been a part of the SBC for one-half of the twentieth century. Programs that began as "pioneer" work and became "new territory" work and then "newer territory" are very much now an integral part of SBC work. This, too, may be forgotten: financial help from various agencies also has been available for those in older parts of the convention.

Mark Arbaugh, the BSU campus minister at Montana Technological University in Butte, began work there as a volunteer and then became a "US-2er" for three years. He and his family were so enthralled with the work that they became volunteers again. The Arbaughs have been in the Big Sky state for eight years. They built a student center and increased the numbers in BSU. That wasn't enough; Mark decided he would also pastor a small church. This is not new work.

An icon among campus ministry state directors is Sam Fort of the Northwest Baptist Convention that includes the states of Oregon, Washington, and a portion of Idaho. Fort, a BSU alumnus from Texas A & M, has lived thirty-one years of his adult life in this section of the world. In his 1995 campus ministries report, the following statistics verified raising the question of calling areas like this convention "newer territory." In this state department there were Fort, two part-time state associates, eight career local campus ministers, three "US-2ers," and twenty semester missionaries (a misnomer—they usual serve a year) and other volunteers.

All of this was accomplished on a budget of $201,000. This convention ranked *twelfth* in reaching students—more than ten thousand—among all state campus-ministry programs in SBC. That should not be called newer work.

Two questions may be raised in this context: Is this where outreach is really going on? Are old convention territory student programs' "holding" patterns taking care of those who are already the group in student centers? The latter question is a dangerous one when considering outreach, evangelism, and church relations.

During the time of transition, living within the parentheses, Christian narcissism, and Baptists' smaller biosphere of the 1980s, the positive program over the convention was in newer territory areas. Leaders at the Baptist Sunday School

Board and HMB found ways to adjust in a time of no direction. Dwindling finances did not deter an ambitious program of short-term volunteerism. Whether or not this becomes a major course of fulfilling ministry needs will be interesting to watch in the future.

CONCLUSION

The climate of the 1980s sapped creativity and innovation. It is difficult to determine if narcissistic values resulted from conservatism or vice-versa. The "me generation" was bred in fertile ground regardless of which view one takes.

During this decade the second generation of campus ministers was nearing retirement. They were the first generation who gave their entire vocational lives to campus ministry. More than age, the "me generation" hastened their retirement plans. Also, this was the time to remove oneself from "the controversy." These campus ministers were the ones the writer of Hebrews could have been thinking the world was not worthy.

The prophetic element historically found in student movements had disappeared and most students were living dogged lives in the academy in pursuit of degrees that would guarantee material wealth. As L. D. Kenney concluded in *The Baptist Program*, "The diploma taken away from the university with them [students] was regarded as a hunting license and not a certificate of arrival."[16] In a time of parenthesis in the 1980s, the faith that students developed was one that discouraged thought—an unbelief masked in piety.

One of perhaps several myths of NSM is that the program was a balanced one. Student work had (and still has) an image problem; it doesn't look as good as it is. NSM never could decide *exactly* who it was trying to reach. Was it single, white undergraduates from ages eighteen to twenty-four? Was it faith seekers alone? Was it new-territory students only? NSM assumed homogeneity instead of diversity. The average age of university students by this time was twenty-five to twenty-six; a large group was married; most worked at least part-time and some forty hours a week. NSM was using old tools for new people.

Another myth is that some have thought student work was a priority of the Baptist Sunday School Board; the truth is it never was. Then in the decade of the 1980s the board gave it less priority. This may be the primary reason for new programming shifts to state convention departments of student work.

A good example of programming shifts is the work of several states on the Atlantic seaboard. These states have joined to have International Student Conferences and campus ministers' meetings—to name two examples. The Eastern Slopes group has accomplished cost cutting since the expense of attending Ridgecrest and Glorieta Student Conferences has risen astronomically. More importantly, this regional identity and consolidation of students makes them feel that they are not alone as followers of Christ. These Atlantic states are securing a volunteer regional coordinator.

One can look at history and graph the growth of campus ministry. In the beginning it was embryonic. From the 1950s to the 1970s, BSU experienced growth in such a way that one cannot resist the cliché—a golden era. As maturity arrived, holding patterns developed. The possible exception was newer territory areas.

Competition developed as other kinds of student ministries came to campuses. Campus Crusade and InterVarsity, along with other groups, became fixtures and diluted the number of participating "BSUers." All of this came at the time of dwindling finances and when NSM, along with state conventions, associations, and churches, was seeking where it could get the most for its dollars. As said by Beverly Thomas-Travis, the United Christian campus minister at Iowa State:

> The financial future is very uncertain for doing campus ministry ecumenically, the momentum has swung "very clearly" to the evangelical groups. I'm astounded by the amount of biblical literalism on a campus of this sort, with its emphasis on science and technology. The more uncertain our individual lives are and the more threatening our society seems to us, the more we turn to traditional texts. We seemed to reach out in time to what our parents and grandparents and great-grandparents accepted as truth because they knew no better.[17]

Although this is from an ecumenist, Thomas-Travis's statement showed that all campus ministry's programs in the 1990s faced lack of moneys. She alluded to another question that is more and more becoming one facing Baptists. Can the church handle the questions and openness of academe? The answer: Not likely. A church like the one previously mentioned near Florida State, which has a minister of students who is trained and works entirely with young, questing minds, may be successful, but certainly represents a minority.

On the whole, however, the climate in churches today creates a crossed sword with the university. The openness of campus life and the dogma of most present-day Baptist churches are contradictory. That is not to deprecate either. The university's task is to raise the questions, and the church's task is to affirm the faith. There is doubt, also, that most churches that deal with all ages of life will concentrate on any one generational gap. Finally, will the different atmospheres of these two institutions allow complete openness or affirmation? The present era is not the time for synthesis of the vocation of the campus minister.

The future expectations may entail a survival mentality, more pressure for numerical results, no new capital investment, fewer full-time staffs, more contract/volunteer workers, tighter management control, more policy decisions, and low toleration for risks. (In the past, workers usually did what they felt right about, and though chastised at times, they were forgiven. Then the code word was *policy*: "I know it doesn't make sense but it's *policy*." Finally, it was "I'm going to do right and hope nobody finds out about it.")

Programming for future needs should be closely aligned with churches. However, the present chasm between the theology that is espoused and biblical theology must be bridged. Perhaps all can take a lesson from the amalgamation of companies in the present business world (Who knows where toothpaste comes from?) as an example of diversifying campus ministry. As a standardized program such as the requirements for Leavell's *First Magnitude,* BSU will not attract but a minority—if any—of today's students.

The glistening of the BSU diamond was tarnished from fires not of Christian students' making. Or was it? In the past they would have changed the *status quo,* but now chose to reflect all that was about them—political and religious conservatism, plus narcissism. Their denomination was in turmoil, but they hardly knew. How could one hope for a better future?

The 1970s had been the "she generation"; the 1980s the "me generation." A hope can be held in the 1990s for a "we generation." There were glimpses of sunshine underneath the dark cloud of the 1980s and early 1990s. University administrators realized they lived in an academic atmosphere that had no community. The task before them is to recover community and reclaim the purpose of the university. That purpose is concern for the *whole* student. Whom did they call to tackle this task? Campus ministers!

Students of the Nineties: An Abandoned Generation?
(Students Seeking an Adequate Faith)

Higher education's constituency had changed, perhaps forever, by the end of the ninth decade of this century. Makeup of the college population had diversified in the early 1980s. This new composition brought not only change but fragmentation. In turn there was a sense of student abandonment by both the academy and church. The higher education scene has lost community.

CONFUSED STUDENTS IN A CONFUSED SOCIETY

Frantic appeals for help began from college administrators in the late 1980s. The Carnegie Foundation first responded with its 1990 report *Campus Life: In Search of Community*. It stated "American higher education is, by almost any measure, a remarkable success. Still, with all our achievements, there are tensions just below the surface and nowhere are the strains of change more apparent than in campus life."[1] Daniel Yankelovich's prediction in 1982 that a slight tremor of value changes below the earth would cause great tremors on the earth had come to pass by the 1990s.

The Carnegie report represents a new beginning of a new integration of education and personhood in the lives of students—a post *in loco parentis* relationship. *In loco parentis* was supposed to have been abandoned in the late 1950s. The cursory conclusion of the report suggests that in a hard-edged, competitive world, more humane and more integrated purposes must be defined. What universities might provide is a new post *in loco parentis* framework of governance in higher education. This segment of society has an important obligation not only to celebrate diversity but also to define more inspired goals. This not only would strengthen the spirit of community on campus but, in so doing, might serve as a model for the nation and the world.[2]

Strengthening the spirit of community on campus demands a new model for campus ministry. Donald G. Shockley, suggested a Corinthian one.[3] This would extend the program of religious student centers to "Corinthian gentile" students who know little about Baptist distinctives and institutionalized Christianity but are urgently seeking God.

This model replaces the historical Athens-Jerusalem one. Athens has been portrayed as the center of knowledge and culture, Jerusalem as the symbol of early Christian communities. The twentieth-century illustration of that polarity has been the relationship between science and religion.

Shockley's suggestion is intriguing. Not only had the apostle Paul come to the shocking conclusion that Jesus amplified Jewish teachings, but he was more surprised that the gentile people of Corinth were among the first to believe. A corollary model is today's campus—Corinthianized, a word the church coined for immorality. Corinth was a party town!

Contemporary students are the children brought into the world during the Archie Bunker era when parental values were thought to be black and white. These students are not the rebels of the 1960s; they are genuinely concerned about spiritual matters, but have no sense of church tradition or practice. Their question is "*how* to be a person of faith, not *why*." Students cannot find God in any of the places they inhabit. They are wandering lost in a spiritual snowstorm, feeling no community, and thus abandoned. Where might they find a community of meaningful being? In fraternity life? Permissive sex and pornographic film? Alcohol? Drugs?

Not only does the Carnegie Foundation report speak to these newer dilemmas but so does William Willimon, chaplain at Duke University. He created a national debate—more correctly, a national "amen"—with his report about walking zombies among today's student bodies.[4]

Amid reports of students studying hard five days and drinking continuously for two days every week, the then new Duke president, Nan Keohane, sensed a lost community. She requested a committee be formed and report on ways of helping rebuild the community on campus. The chaplain was chairperson.

Four conclusions came from his committee's thirty-two-page report titled "We Work Hard, We Play Hard":

1. Most Duke undergraduates seemed to believe the university was "merely a step on the way to law school, a necessary evil to be endured before Wall Street."

2. Many top student scholars at Duke were dissatisfied with the campus's intellectual life. Twelve women who left in 1991 said their reason for leaving was the "anti-intellectual climate."

3. Alcohol was the number one problem concerning public safety and student health.

4. Students complained that they rarely saw their professors outside the classroom. Professors said they stayed out of students' lives because they wanted "to allow them to be adults."[5]

If Keohane wanted to know if student life was contributing to a loss of community and was hindering the academic process, the answer was a resounding *yes!* In only four decades academe had moved from *in loco parentis* to near abandonment of its students.

The suggestion in the Carnegie report was for a post *in loco parentis*; the suggestion from Willimon's complete report was "Let's be friends." They were almost the same.

What an opportunity for campus ministry! Yet, there is irony in all this. The campus minister who is seeking to rescue students in this snowstorm of abandonment is a citizen of all three cities—Athens, Jerusalem, and now, Corinth—but is not at home in any! The mind, the church, and the world beckon her or him as a campus leader now in an ambiguous position.

As despicable as the word *dysfunctional* is (especially when it comes to family life, for what family doesn't have some form of dysfunctionality?), it describes students. They are not interested in what freedom truly is—freedom sounds too much like liberalism. They have little or no sense of history or the continuity of life. One sees this most pitifully in race relations. (Race relations have reverted to earlier animosity and have lost some of the 1960s gains.) Yet, underneath it all, their psyches crave stability and relationship. Perhaps these feelings of despair do not belong only to students; there is reason to believe the adult population loses hope also. Why do books like Thomas Moore's *Care of the Soul* and *Soulmates* make the best-seller lists along with William Bennett's *The Book of Virtues*? What about the popularity of James Redfield's New Age works, *The Celestine Prophecy* and *The Tenth Insight*, that in the final analysis are only pop psychology? These books speak to an American public who are seeking a spiritual *raison d'être*.

Aristotle believed that it was impossible to teach anything important to people who are not your friends. Only friends have the privilege of hurting you in the right way. Faculty have been guilty of *overdistancing*, to use Sharon Parks's word in *The Critical Years: The Young Adult Search for a Faith to Live by*. While it may be appropriate for young people to try new ideas without coercion, faculty members too often virtually ignore contemporary students.

Another irony in trying to move from *in loco parentis* is that universities, never in forty years, have emerged with any theory of campus governance to replace that historic concept. At a loss as to who should lead, administrators sidestepped rather than confronted the issues. While university officials understood their authority had forever changed, this shift was not understood, or accepted, by either parents or the public. Even state legislators and the courts were not willing to excuse the university.

That was why William Willimon's Duke report struck a nerve of the nation's universities. In view of all the consternation, he sought conversation with and corresponding comments of the Student Affairs Committee seeking "damage control," especially about alcohol on campus. His recorded conversation was as follows:

> I [Willimon] blurted out, "Can't something be done about this? Don't you think it is a shame that these people come to us with such potential and then waste themselves with alcohol?"

A dean responded, "But what can we do? After all, we are not their parents."

"We are not their parents," I agreed, "but could we at least be their older brothers and sisters? Could we be their friends?"

"Might the modern university consider playing the role not of a substitute parent but of a wise friend," I wondered.

"It is important that we give students their freedom," many respond.

"Freedom is developmentally important. We need to treat students like adults, relying on them to make mature decisions for themselves."

But students are not adults. At best a student is, in Daniel Levinson's words, "a novice adult" (*The Seasons of a Man's Life*, 1979). Few students are capable of "making their own decisions" or "think for themselves." Leaving them to themselves, with no skills for discernment, meager personal experience and a narrow worldview, they become the willing victim of the most totalitarian form of government devised—namely, a submission to their peers, obeisance to people just like them.[6]

This long quotation has compactness. Willimon has captured a microcosm of student abandonment in the 1990s. In retrospect, very little confusion would have happened during the 1950s when universities began distancing themselves from the philosophy *in loco parentis*. The reason is simple: Though suddenly freed from imposed living values already learned, 1950 students were not going to become different people.

"In place of parents" will never be reinstated. Today's university setting is not consistent with "university" as defined. Academe is a multiversity, not only in curriculum, but also different types of students. Ways and organizations must be found to create unified value systems that give 1990s' students not only a sense of learning but also a reason for being.

A CONTEMPORARY STUDENT PROFILE

Contemporary students are victims of low self-esteem that causes fear of decision making and lack of awareness of others. The fear of decision making expresses itself in delayed marriages, which in turn has given America a new phrase—the "boomerang family." After university days the offspring returns to the nest.

Jack Greever, former director of the Division of Student Work for the Baptist General Convention of Texas, presented this profile of contemporary students:

. . . students of today have been baby-sat, taught and nurtured by the television set, becoming at the same time both the most information saturated and the most illiterate of generations. . . . the latter especially regarding history, literature, art, music, and religion.

To summarize, the student of today needs affirmation and a positive self-image, needs to be focused with a sense of purpose.[7]

To counteract this deficient profile, students need to realize most of the characteristics stated rob them of full lives. As Christ exhorted, "The thief comes only to steal and kill and destroy. I came that they may have life, and have it abundantly" (John 10:10, NRSV).

CONCLUSION

A few individual lessons the 1990s students need to learn, or relearn, are the purpose of Christian vocation, the wonders of human sexuality, and the exhilaration of friendship, but the most important thing they need is to ascertain the will of God. These other lessons will follow. Don Hammonds recalled, "In the fifties, as students, we spent a lot of time wondering what God's will was for our lives. Today's students spend a lot of time telling God where He is going to fit in their lives."

As important as it is to question students about their Christian challenges, one needs to pause and ask denominations what challenge is forthcoming for their campus-ministry organizations. One can almost graph the historical growth of Southern Baptist campus ministry: From the embryonic Leavell years to the golden era of 1950s and 1960s growth to the present, the experience of maturity has led to holding patterns of past programming in the confines of Baptist student centers. New ways of outreach are the beckoning opportunities for struggling novice adults of the 1990s. The traditional ways of the past will no longer do.

David Hazelwood, an expert leader of management and a futurist, was a former consultant for NSM. He has an interesting concept of finding new ways to package old products. There is no reason to believe that even "old products" like Baptist campus ministry, the church, and—yes, even the faith—shouldn't always be looking for "new packaging."

Hazelwood has used the illustration of the ways the Arm and Hammer Company has retargeted soda carbonate. Soda carbonate was once used only for cooking. One morning someone didn't have any toothpaste, so he used baking soda. Why not put it in toothpaste? Another person noted that soda carbonate had a way of decreasing odors in cooking areas. Refrigerators developed odors. Why not get homemakers to put boxes of baking soda in them? In an era when competition has crept in, moneys are decreasing, and downsizing is the order of the day, Baptist campus ministries could take lessons from a baking soda company.

Daniel Vestal, recently elected as the second executive director of the Cooperative Baptist Fellowship, expressed the need of repackaging from a church perspective. He remarked when addressing the fellowship:

> If we are going to have a missionary legacy, we are going to have to distinguish between *centrifugal* and *centripetal* forces in Jesus' Great Commission. Jesus commanded Christians to be an outward-moving force—a *centrifugal* force—to reach the world, not an inward-moving *centripetal* force that results in the self-absorbed life characteristic of so many churches.[8]

The same warning should be heeded by Baptist Student Unions.

The BSU diamond, which sparkled so brilliantly in earlier years, is being chipped and scratched and is losing luster because of the struggle to adjust to a new type of student in an "information highway" society. What new horizons are developing for this tenth decade type of young person? Are "spiritual care" organizations, including Baptist campus ministry, sufficient for the day? Certainly not without challenge, creativity, customizing, cooperating, and courage for developing an unknown future.

The Future of Baptist Campus Ministry
(Speeding into the Twenty-First Century)

Like ecotones created when fresh waters from southern streams meet the salt waters of the Gulf of Mexico, campus ministries and the verities of faith must find ways to meet the technological world of the twenty-first century. Will campus ministries be "snail mail" or "E-mail?" The faith that filters technological worlds will be the faith that endures. What new programming will occur as the 1990s student seeks the "how" to God?

Five words—*caring, creativity, customizing, cooperating,* and *challenge*—may hold the key as to how campus ministry will program as the race toward the twenty-first century accelerates.

Baptist campus ministry will, hopefully, have new emphases. At the same time, there may be programmatic activities, some forgotten, that need reclaiming for contemporary students. Contemporary students are different. They drop out. They change majors. Some are in the fifth decade of life wrestling with career changes. Some are parents with empty nests that allow them to complete their education. Students are conservative, politically correct, and no longer denominationally minded. Students are different, but that difference may offer the opportunity for placing new wine in new wineskins.

These pursuers of educational dreams include the nation's largest minorities, Hispanics and African Americans, who need special attention because integration is ongoing. International students still look upon the United States as the preeminent place to be educated. Yet, total education is not achieved without international visitors wrestling with the globe's Creator.

CAMPUS MINISTRY CLAIMING THE FUTURE

Can Baptist campus ministry cope with these complex mixes of people? It can if the current leaders are *challengers—caring and creative*—who are willing to *customize* Baptist Student Unions. Also, because of the current controversy in SBC, leadership and students must determine how much *cooperation* is going to be maintained with integrity. This calls both groups to *courageous* Christian living on the edges of the faith.

Caring

The greatest challenge is the courage to look anew at evangelism as a whole lifestyle instead of an isolated incident. Too long have campus ministry people seen evangelism in isolation.

Having still not understood the full import of death and resurrection, the remaining apostles asked, ". . . is this the time when you will restore the kingdom to Israel?" (Acts 1:6, NRSV). Not wanting to chide their narrowness, Christ replied, "It is not for you to know the times or periods that the Father has set by his own authority. . . . you will receive power when the Holy Spirit has come upon you; and *you will be my witness* [italics mine] in Jerusalem, in all Judea and Samaria and to the ends of the earth" (Acts 1:7-8, NRSV).

This revelation—you will be my witness—still needs clarification and amplification today. Simply, *witnessing* means *Christians care*. Students are witnesses. They may be good or bad at it, depending on whether they really care or just want to put another notch on their salvation guns.

One-on-one witnessing, personal evangelism, still has its place. However, both people and theology may wrestle with its definition. There are serious questions about "Roman Road," "zap," tract, and kinds of evangelism that confront. The "born-again" experience is only the beginning. The real conclusion is what one becomes and not what one does. From the initial experience with the Christ come two vital characteristics: caring and friendship.

Perhaps, Christians need to recall their own conversions. As they look back, most find it is not an all-consuming, final experience. They still have much to learn and, in learning, never question their initial experience. Frederick Buechner explained better:

> To say I was born again, to use the traditional phrase, is to say too much. I remained, in most ways, as self-centered after the fact as I was before and, God knows, remain so still. But in another way, to say that I was born again is to say too little. Just like elusive fireflies in the twilight of evening, there have been not a few moments when times went beyond time. These moments caused that which was mysterious, precious, and all consuming to enter my soul in the dusks of life.[1]

A more than cursory look at the New Testament epistles will astonish most Christians. When the dual words *Savior* and *Lord* are both present, *Lord* always takes precedence. (The apostle Peter seemed especially fond of this progression. See 2 Pet. 1:11, 2:20, 3:2 and 18, NRSV.) Giving God through Jesus Christ life's lordship is proof the Christ is Savior too. To say "Jesus saved me" when one's life does not give evidence of lordship is probably erroneous. Too much emphasis is being made by individuals and churches concerning the initial encounter with God. New Testament scholar Frank Stagg wrote of salvation being a gift and demand. Thomas Merton's brilliant phrase of "my continuous conversion, continuous autobiography" should haunt seekers through the ages.

Salvation—a gift it is! Following the divine command to all Christians to seek sheep for the Shepherd is proof of their received gift. The continuous autobiography of caring is evidence of continuous, ongoing conversion.

Caring has begun when students meet God for the first time; friendship begins simultaneously, yet it continues through the Christian maturation process. The maturation of young Christians is one of the greatest strengths of Baptist Student Unions. Although friendship and caring are close synonyms, caring begins with the evangel's message of the Savior to nonchristian collegians. Both friendship and caring matures.

William Bennett, secretary of education in President Reagan's cabinet, said this:

> Friendships usually rise out of mutual interests and common aims, and these are strengthened by the benevolent impulses that sooner or later grow. The demands for friendship—for frankness, for self-revelation, for taking friends' criticism as seriously as their expressions of admiration or praise, for stand-by-me loyalty, and for assistance at the point of sacrifice—are all potent encouragements to *moral maturation* [italics mine] and even ennoblement.[2]

This is the type of friendship that students need from faculty and administration, as William Willimon was insisting. Lifestyle evangelism assumes caring friendships. University friendships tell parents which way their children are leaning, and what better place than involvement in Christian organizations can young people send good signals home?

Students of the 1990s are different, but as in every other era, they need care through friendships of lifestyle evangelicals. BSU programs need creativity to meet these low-self-esteemed youngsters who are radically different from their parents—even from their student predecessors.

Creativity

If Arthur Levine, president of Bradford College, is correct in saying that contemporary students are going first class on the Titanic and if Allan Bloom, former professor at the University of Chicago, is right about how higher education has impoverished the souls of today's students, then successful Baptist campus ministers are going to have to be unusually creative people. Creativity is an activity producing results that are novel, useful, and understandable.[3]

Students shouldn't have the same BSU experience for four years; they should have a different BSU experience each year! Valid criticism has been observed in what is titled "freshmen" Baptist Student Unions. Freshman Baptist Student Unions are those who only keep students for a year, or two at the most. Superior campus ministry programs benefit students throughout their college careers. Freshman programs are usually one-activity programs. Evangelism, Bible study, or missions usually constitute the entire BSU atmosphere. This program attracts only one type of student, usually immature, who does not intend to change from his or her Jerusalem of the past.

Campus ministers who are creative have a depth mentality and are divergent thinkers. They think internationally so they usually have a worldview. They think as freshmen think, but also relate to graduate student concerns. They are at home with rural, suburban, and city students and with pastors. With Baptist students who feel abandoned by their institutions, collegiate and church, and with their denomination living in a smaller biosphere, today's denominational student leaders realize programming needs customizing.

Customizing

Customizing includes continually looking for new things to do with programming and also recovering and adopting some good old ideas. Campus ministry needs the recovery of vocational emphasis and weeks of love, courtship, and marriage emphasis. Different terminology may be needed, but the concepts are still important.

The educational task concerning evangelism should be reconsidered also. Just because this task has been backward in the past—saviorhood without lordship—does not invalidate introducing students to the central figure of the Christian faith. If telling students about the vocation of work and/or how to have a marvelous marriage is all there is to say, then campus ministers will neglect the motivating concept that will cause them to be successful in work and marriage.

Customizing is the activity of deciding what students need at a given time, a particular year, or in a particular geographical area. Customizing also means that every program in a state convention should not be the same in every geographical area. In a state like Louisiana where the northern part has Baptists like kudzu and where in the southern part Roman Catholics are in the same proportion, BSU should not program the same way on every campus. Neither should the state's leadership expect the same results. A state BSU director has a tremendous burden in deciding what results should be sought on each campus, but he/she must.

Customizing in the 1990s is much more than geographical. Every campus has common needs, but each campus will also have peculiar ones. At least four categories may be common to all (yet not necessarily so): religious freedom as a Baptist distinctive, the vocation of work, minority ministries, and issues of sexuality. Addressing these categories of need could begin to fill the vacuum created by students' feelings of abandonment.

Religious Freedom. Religious freedom is being threatened seriously in America. When Chief Justice Rehnquist of the U.S. Supreme Court continually has said and written that he sees no wall of separation between church and state, Baptists of this country are in serious difficulty. Especially are they threatened in relation to the First Amendment of the Constitution and to the vision of Patrick Henry and James Madison under a tree agreeing that state and church in this young country would always be separate blurs, a position that vindicated the persecuted Baptist preachers in Virginia.

Baptists have never bowed to creeds (confessions, yes! Jesus is Lord!). *Bible* freedom has always been interpreted as the priesthood of the believer and not the authority of government or pastor. *Soul* freedom means individuals will be judged only by God. Judgment will be not only for Baptists but for all of humanity. *Church* freedom is in the universal church Jesus prayed for in John 17. The apostle Paul speaks about freedom for the Colossae and Ephesus churches. The Baptist believer's church may be local in nature, but it is part of the universal one also.

Religious freedom is threatened in other ways: by reconstructionism that causes one not to see the cross because it is wrapped in the flag or by New Age people who are delighted with psychological gadflies like James Redfield and his books. America's collegians are looking for spiritual (little "s") answers without responsibility. The nation and its churches are victims of a shallow spirituality that will not hold when cherished historical freedoms are questioned.

Baptist Student Unions must find ways to combat threats to religious freedoms. A tremendous amount of customizing will be demanded if Baptist distinctives are brought back into BSU curriculums. The omission of teaching what a Baptist believes may be the reason contemporary students lack commitment to a local congregation.

This is the challenge for modern-day Baptist campus ministry. Students should be convinced that the joyous Christian life is so because they are free! "Then Jesus said to the Jews who had *believed* [italics mine] in him, 'If you continue in my word, you are truly my disciples; and you will know the truth, and the truth will make you *free* [italics mine]'" (John 8:31–32, NRSV).

Work and the Will of God. William Hall Preston, as associate Southwide secretary, came to assist Leavell in 1928. He stayed in this position until his retirement. One of his duties was to promote Vocational Emphasis Week among fledgling BSU programs in the South.

Preston's favorite phrase about vocations was "Follow your bent." He meant for students to find their God-given talents and assume those talents would help them find God's will vocationally. This concept was broad and inclusive: It did not imply that God's call was only for those pursuing religious vocations. It included everyone. This concept needs to be recovered for today's students and may be a part of the customizing process of Baptist student programs.

Young men first wanted to be cowboys (until Willie Nelson's "Mothers, Don't Let Your Boy's Grow up To Be Cowboys"), then firefighters or athletes. As they grew older, they realized the question "What do you want to be?" was not about jobs and pay, but about life. The question should be posed not as what do you do *for* a living but as what do you do *with* your living.

William Bennett reminded everyone, "Life's greatest joys are not what one does apart from the work of one's life, but with the work of one's life. There are no menial jobs, only menial attitudes."[4]

Students who view university days as drudgeries on the way to riches are on the skateboard to oblivion. No students are completely enlisted in BSU, or the Christian faith, until they feel themselves in the center of God's will. This emphasis provides a sure way out of feelings of abandonment for contemporary students. They need the euphoria of the Israelites returning from exile to rebuild the walls of Jerusalem for they had a mind to work.

Ethnic Minorities. Does anyone have the right to discuss ethnic minorities? It often seems like trying to get one's hands on Jell-O. Speakers seem to both irritate and ostracize all groups in an audience by the time they finish speaking on this topic. One must be careful when attempting to comment on a part of the populace as diverse and complex as ethnics.

However, in looking at the statistics, particularly at African-American and Hispanic enrollments in universities, the reaction is "Speakers are not the only ones having trouble!" The percentage of African-American high school graduates going to college actually *dropped* from 40 percent in 1976 to 30 percent in 1988; for low-income Hispanics, the college participation rate fell from 50 percent in 1976 to 35 percent in 1988.[5]

Especially does tension rise when race relations of the 1950s are discussed in relation to the places where white southerners participated. Many gambled their church vocations and, thereby, jeopardized their families in support of equal opportunities for all. Young African Americans today, on the whole, have little sense of history. Yet, they clamor for black studies in universities' curricula.

Perhaps some (this author included) were wrong by not supporting African Americans having their separate religious groups within Baptist Student Unions on predominantly white campuses. Those who did, especially Baptist campus minister William Lee, formerly at the University of Tennessee, had an entree with African-American students. At this time, however, others felt that type of activity violated their Christian sensitivity toward racial segregation.

One must agree with Scott Hudgins, former US-2 campus minister at Columbia University and now director of Baptist Studies at Emory University in Atlanta:

> It is my contention that African-American students for the most part are seeking ways to express their faith in such a manner which affirms their sense of cultural identity, however it may be defined. Perhaps not since the late 1960-1970s has there been such a pronounced sense of racial ethnic consciousness evident among students of color on college campuses. In addition, it is not unusual for such a consciousness to be manifest in terms of a nationalistic/separatist ideology. In such an environment, many students are often seeking to develop as integrative faith expression, one that is authentically African and Christian.[6]

Here is another form of customizing programs that needs to occur in the last years of the millennium for Baptist students. Campus ministers must be open to change while not compromising their integrity.

New Looks at Human Sexuality. Who does not remember the hop, skip, and jump of the heart when "BSUers" realized that once again it was time for the annual Love, Courtship, and Marriage Week at the BSU center? The most cherished hopes were wrapped in God's will for lives vocationally in order to achieve the next goal: a family. The primary struggle was the high expectation of finding a godly spouse. Alas, one does wonder if that is a goal of contemporary academicians.

Older people must admit that nearing the close of the twentieth century the "rules" are not that simple. In the midst of the struggle for women's equality, one can hear the exclamation of fathers of yesteryear when hearing for the first time the phrase "women's equality": "Equality! They have always been *superior!*"

Some come to the issue of gender equality with awe and sheer exaltation at the otherness of the opposite sex. This does not mean, however, that any individual should demand equal opportunity in areas where they are not competent. Just being one sex or the other is not a qualification for anything. Equal or superior ability, regardless of gender, is what demands serious consideration in the workplace and everywhere else.

Equal opportunity, however, should still be given those who have been denied such opportunity. Donald Shockley admits that the church is not exactly leading the charge in this area, but that women can learn a lesson from the Civil Rights movement. Getting to the lunch counter is a hollow victory if nothing on the menu is appealing. It is not enough just to get the door open; she must be able to come in without parking her identity outside.[7]

This is not the place to take time for a discussion of correct biblical interpretation. However, good interpretation does not give equal weight to every biblical injunction. Therefore, biblical restrictions like ". . .women should be silent in the churches" (1 Cor. 14:34, NRSV)—which is probably illustrative only for a particular woman in the church at Corinth—are lifted for women in Gal. 3:27–28: "As many of you as were baptized into Christ have clothed yourselves with Christ. There is no longer slave or free, there is no longer male and female; for all are one in Christ Jesus" (NRSV).

Other issues of human sexuality demand that present BSU programs need customizing. For example, in discussing abortion, why is there not more focus on questions of premarital and other-than-marital sex? The high divorce rate across the nation is linked to these extramarital sexual activities. The word *adultery* has escaped students' vocabularies and with it has gone the word *trust*. Lack of trust in marriage often begins with previous nonbiblically sanctioned sexual activity.

No discussion of new looks at human sexuality can close without the subject of homosexuality. This issue, like the one of ethnic minorities, is so confusing and has people so polarized that good answers are hard to confirm. However, to say

AIDS is God's execution of homosexuals seems to deny all the explicit teaching of Jesus concerning care and compassion. No one decided one day to choose his or her sexual orientation! Scientific data is suggesting more and more that homosexuality has genetic origins.

Because homosexuality has become more open, current campus ministers will find themselves confronted with this issue. (Could those "sissy males" and "tomboy females" of the 1950s have been the homosexual group?) Will campus ministers give the same loving counsel to homosexual children of God as they give to all others?

Confronting the whole issue of human sexuality with students who have considerably more tomorrows than yesterdays will determine family values of the future. With students who feel abandoned on today's campuses, the challenge of trying to customize a relevant program on human sexuality is of major significance. Customizing current programs for campus ministry is a must, but only after the leaders determine how caring and creative they, themselves, are.

Cooperating

Someone, somewhere, solemnly said that there is no one more dangerous than a person with only one idea. That statement characterizes the atmosphere in Baptist religious life today.

Cooperation was easier to get in the past; if fact, one wonders how long it would have taken for the hierarchy to realize a campus minister wasn't on the job. If permission wasn't granted to do what they wished, campus religious workers could bank on the truism "It's easier to get forgiveness than permission." That is not so today.

Assuming that universities are wakening to the possibilities of developing more community spirit, cooperation awaits the campus minister to be a part of these endeavors. Universities have expanded community services and staffs: counselors, financial-aid officers, and residence-hall supervisors. By cooperating with these folk, campus ministers can reach students *on* campus who need the central figure of the Christian faith. These students may never find their way to the Baptist student center. Campus ministers' stationery should carry the reminder that BSU is "a Christian ministry to the academic community." This assumption *to* means *toward* which in turn means *on* campus.

Because of the rigid religious atmosphere among Southern Baptists today, communication is cooperation at its best. If campus ministers are courageous enough to stretch the parameters of the faith about the issues of the day, they may need strong support from pastors and immediate superiors to quiet criticism from the rank and file of church and town. Those who have knowledge of the campus minister's dedication, worth, and program are going to be there to intercede when the waters get turbulent. Sound reasons for a campus minister's work may make perimeter people realize that they haven't thought about those realms, or areas, which are the campus worker's responsibility.

The future isn't bright for those who are used to a "freewheeling" type of ministry. Campus ministers should in the future expect more rigid planning processes, tighter management controls, no reduction in policy decisions, less tolerance for risks, and less leadership from the Sunday School Board Student Ministry Department.

Challenge

The present is a silent time for campus ministers to be more challenged that they are within God's plan for their lives. Too many times the phrase "God led me to do this or that" has been an excuse for shoddy work. Integrity with God and students seems to be more of a necessity in troubled times. Southern Baptists need to think of building bridges over the troubled waters of dissension.

There may come a time in the future when campus personnel and church hierarchy cannot cooperate in a biosphere that becomes smaller and smaller. Not only will the doctrinal biosphere become smaller, more rigid, but it also may be less Baptistic. Campus ministers who lose integrity and feel a loss of worthiness will pass this on to their students. Instead of these feelings happening, other avenues of professional service will open for the great, good, and gracious God. At the end of the rainbow in the heavens, one can feel him smiling on those facing this predicament.

CONCLUSION

A dismal assessment of the present does not mean ultimate chaos or doom. Prophecy is unpredictable. Futurists today are suggesting that those involved in Southern Baptist life not make forecasts. Campus ministers may make assumptions, but if those prove to be untrue, they had better be resilient enough to alter them quickly.

Where is SBC going? No one knows. Walter Shurden has written, "Baptists are not a silent people." There has always been controversy in this denomination, but even Shurden has not known one like this. It has become so institutionalized and personalized that most cannot refrain from taking sides. The denomination continues to exist, but a large segment has chosen to work within SBC as the Cooperative Baptist Fellowship, particularly, and in other groups, generally.

It appears that SBC faces years of conflict. Its growth will probably stagnate and, consequently, decline in financial strength. In relation to student ministry, this implies challenge, courage, flexibility, and a renewed dedication to the task.

There will be a greater variety of students and more competition from other campus religious organizations; there used to be only a handful, but now it is easy to count almost thirty. There will be fewer paid personnel, more use of bivocational and volunteer persons, shorter budgets, and less building. This does not mean less opportunity for effectiveness; it means student work will be different from its historical past.

All students need God in various ways—to be "saved," to become more mature, and to find His will for their lives. One hope "the controversy" may give is that Baptist history, polity, and doctrine may cause an interest among students and through them these singular distinctions of Baptists will recover.

The 1990s is a demanding and exhilarating time to be involved in campus ministry. For the third generation of Southern Baptist campus ministers, it may be the worst of times and the best of times; it is a time of foolishness, but it could be a time of wisdom.

The most important things will not change—the human condition, God's love and power, and Jesus' presence and compassion. This is enough to give student ministry hope—Christian hope. Happy seventy-fifth anniversary!

"The Wind Blows Where It Chooses . . ."
(The Great, Good, Gracious God)

Everyone involved in campus ministry should see the 1996 movie *Mr. Holland's Opus*. In it Richard Dreyfuss embodies the meaning of what great teachers should be. The classic line was Dreyfuss exclaiming, "If you do away with the budget for music, drama, and the other arts, there will be no reason to budget for reading and writing because there won't be anything to read and write about!"

The movie is an illustration of the best in campus ministers. Its classic line is an implied warning to those who may think of curtailing student-ministry money. Southern Baptist leadership will mightily suffer if their base for leadership is diminished. What students become as adults after college is proof of the type of work campus ministers do while students are in college.

It has been very difficult to write a philosophical history, but this type of history is paramount. Movements demand a *raison d'être*. I resisted the temptation to write about the successes and the people who caused one of Southern Baptists' greatest movements to be so influential. John Moore, state student director in Louisiana, shared an experience he had at the Baptist FMB. He and similar colleagues listened to an official in the personnel department say that almost 90 percent of Southern Baptists' foreign missionaries have BSU experience as part of their résumés. The joyful and surely more interesting task of writing about successes as these—and others—will be left to others.

THREE GENERATIONS OF CAMPUS MINISTERS

Since the first generation of Baptist campus student workers began, each has offered talents to make this program the diamond it has become after seventy-five years. Two of them have passed into history. What does God have in store for the present generation? Will it leave a legacy as the others?

The BSU Secretary
The first generation, for most, did not represent many years. The participants were young men looking for a type of work that provided a stepping stone to a collegiate church or they were young women who soon married. Yet, both made the initial thrust for campus religious life. Their lives and names became

catchwords of the movement. They were giants who did not fear to tread toward the unknown land called academia.

Most of them, directly or otherwise, were chosen by Frank Leavell to pursue his dream. He taught them his philosophy. The program from 1922 until Leavell's death in 1949 was more successful than even he envisioned. The leaders were mostly untrained, but they were dedicated. Lest we forget, there were even those before the secretaries—names long forgotten and lost in history. Christian lay-persons—in town and on campus—were volunteers who waited for someone fulltime, but did not let the light of Christ dim among students in the meantime.

For the last decade, I have challenged newer territory workers with illustrations of volunteer workers in the older convention areas as late as the 1940s. I explained it took almost half a century for the past generation's contribution to be recognized. Betsy Draper of Boston responded, "I hope it doesn't take us that long!" That is my hope too.

Directors of Student Ministries

The second generation was first titled "BSU directors" then "directors of student ministries." Though not officially voted upon by the state student directors until 1970, I used the term early in 1950. It was in this decade that seminary-trained individuals were solidifying a vocation. Keegan's study commissions had much to do with adding luster to the content of our work. Some of us made our reputations during this period. Students following World War II were responsible in all areas of their Christian lives. Battling racial segregation of the South was one example. These students were of high moral character. It was easy to do student work.

During this period the concept of short-term missions developed. This is the unique innovation of student work until the present. In the fiftieth anniversary of short-term missions (1995) according to the annual student report from Nashville, 27,056 participated in some form of short-term work. Members of Baptist Student Unions also contributed $3,286,281 to this cause.[1]

The unified philosophical statement was adopted by the state student directors as a result of the work of the six commissions and two study groups for the development of objectives, nomenclature, and membership for Baptist campus-ministry programs. All of this work, along with doing away with *in loco parentis*, caused directors of student ministries to begin thinking in terms of a lifelong vocation.

By the early 1980s, some were retiring having never worked anywhere for Baptists except on campuses around the nation. We have lived through what Jesse Fletcher called in his sesquicentennial history, *The Great Advance*. The second generation took Leavell's embryonic ideas and ideals to create the largest student religious movement in America.

What started in 1979 as a split between theological moderate-conservatives and fundamentalists in SBC developed into the largest schism this body has known in 151 years. It continues to cast a pall on *all* the activities of this great body even now, and student work has not been excluded. Retirement saved most of the second generation from the agonies of self-righteousness.

The Campus Minister

There is no evidence of a specific time when title terminology changed, again, to *campus minister.* Perhaps leaders realized that ministry was what we did. Also, the title added prestige, placing religious workers on a level playing field with other adults on campus. At last the opposition to the term disappeared—one that was never coherent in the first place. Some had argued the term was evidence of no program. That could not have been further from truth in Southern Baptist student ministry.

The third generation now called campus ministers are finding themselves living in a smaller biosphere of Baptist life. "The controversy" tightens activities of Baptist Student Unions like rings on a barrel—the rings seemingly smaller and tighter each year. "Safe" programs are the norm and the inward Christian-life programs seem to be all that matters. In 1995 student gifts for hunger declined—an evidence of the lack of outward concern. However, hopefully, there are some Baptist Student Unions that don't fit this description.

We need not think that this seemingly lasting of "the controversy" will be the decline of Southern Baptists' campus ministry. There is need to be diligent in this series of "nows" to see that does not happen. "All we can do is try to live one now at a time without getting too worked up about the last now or the next now," said a character in the contemporary novel *The Horse Whisperer.*[2]

Because of dwindling finances at every level of denominational life, those who gaze at budgets may be tempted to look at campus-ministry items and muse, "Here is some 'soft' money we can safely cut." If this seeming economy emerges, a dire warning must follow: Don't mortgage tomorrow's future denominational, missionary, and local church leadership for a present quick fix. BSU's function as incubator for the future will not be easily replaced and must not be sacrificed.

Charles Lillard, in his 1995 presidential address at the Association of Southern Baptist Campus Ministers speaking as an "aging" BSU director, reminded us that campus ministry belongs to students. "It is a student movement. If our convention or association kills it, it will be resurrected again by the ones who began it in the first place. Only an aging BSU director could know that."[3] At a Haystack Prayer meeting nestled on a hillside, a group of students did just that in 1806, and if necessary, they will do it again.

FUTURE STUDENT TRENDS

Futurists warn in today's world that no one should be bold enough to prophesy. Trends on the current information highway may dwindle as yesterday's mistakes. We should not make too many forecasts, or assumptions, or else we should be able to alter all programming quickly. Don't place future student trends in concrete.

Today's students are different. Yet, they have the same characteristics of all novice adults through the ages in higher education. The human spirit changes only as it is filtered through the sieves of God. Some students are invaders, more are tourists, many are refugees, and, surely, we are still in the business of developing pilgrims. The invaders of BSU programs act as if God has particularly called them to change everything even to "saving" the campus minister. BSU tourists are those who delight in the social life of the organization, but have little to do with the spiritual emphasis of the program. Refugees are those who have suffered early in life and experience religious doubt, death, or divorce that so often fragments family life and circles of friends. Christian pilgrims are those we depend upon to show the best in Baptist Student Unions. Perhaps the more students change, the more they remain the same, yet demographic, sociological, moral, and religious trends of the 1990s make students different; therefore, religious programs must be different.

Demographic Trends

The percentage of traditional-age students will decline. College reports now say the average age of students is twenty-six to twenty-eight years, and it is more than probable that students above this age will be in the majority within a decade. More women will make up the student body than men. That means that BSU's historical tendency on traditional college campuses to enlist more women than men will only increase. Ethnic groups—African American, Asians, Hispanics—will grow faster than all other segments of the student population. There will be an increase in older people who desire career changes, who are divorced, or who are single parents.

Sociological Trends

Greater tolerance, more choices, and a wide range of acceptable behavior will encourage individualism. This encourages programming toward Christian character maturation. The pluralistic society shows changes ethnically, in family forms, lifestyles, and interests. We need to go back and look at some of the programs of the 1950s and 1960s and focus on specific needs of specific groups. The generalist approach, if ever it was *in*, is now definitely *out*.

Sociological trends tell us that women's roles will expand, but, along with that expansion, will come social and personal stress. Also, family life will continue to be shattered by death and divorce. I have already suggested a return to programs majoring on a return to community. Campus ministers must develop family and marriage skills.

Moral Trends

Moral trends reflect sociological trends. AIDS may cause a small decrease in sexual freedom, but sexual openness will continue because of its emphasis in the mass communications media. The possible legalization of certain drugs will likely cause more use, and campus ministers need again to educate students concerning accepting Christian responsibility about the uses of their bodies.

Cautionary flags are waving. The answer to these problems is not in organizations like the Christian Coalition. The use of biblical principles should develop positive images of the Christian life. Many moral issues have been so politicized that the general populace has forgotten where moral issues originally formed. I do not want to think the Christian faith is the only source of morality, though it is a major one. Yesteryear's philosophers, ethicists, poets, and other creators of original thought made their contribution.

The negatives of the Christian Right have dimmed the positiveness of Jesus of Nazareth who is the example of the way, the truth, and reality of life. Follow him!

Religious Trends

Today's religious life reflects the sociological trends of the moment. Today's Baptist students no longer pride themselves about a great denomination. They have forgotten, or were never taught, their heritage. They dabble their toes in many different religious groups seeking an adequate faith. Religious affiliation has more to do with style than the worship of the great, good, and gracious God. Baptist heritage needs recovering—smilingly, for some of us decried the "separateness" of Baptists long ago when we never acted in concert with the other people of God.

If true Baptist heritage is recovered, disillusionment with organized religion will cease to grow. One style of worship that has caused the cynicism about institutionalized religion is the religious pornography of several prominent evangelists in recent years—among them Jimmy Swaggert and Jim Bakker. The exception is Billy Graham. Yet this phenomenon is habit forming when some students do not get out of bed to worship. If disillusionment with organized religion does not change, today's students will be lost from tomorrow's church.

WHITHER SOUTHERN BAPTIST CAMPUS MINISTRY?

The seventy-fifth anniversary of Southern Baptists' student ministry finds the denomination at crossroads. The direction we take may or may not bode well for BSU. Campus ministry is expensive. History tells us, however, that per capita results may make it the least expensive long-term investment. The leadership of Southern Baptists' administrative, missionary, scholarly, and pastoral roots began in campus ministries across the nation.

A new type of leadership graces the top echelons of agencies, seminaries, and state conventions. They may be pharaohs who remember not the Josephs of BSU work. If so, a vacuum for leadership will result. The time is challenging and certain clouds darken the horizon. Campus leadership will demand people of deep dedication with a great need for flexibility.

Even with restructuring and reorganization imminent, "the controversy" continues with no end in sight. The future probably means more splintering among several groups within the convention. SBC will grow more slowly and perhaps even decline. This result could not have come at a worse time.

The population most attracted to SBC churches is declining; the birth rate of these folks is low. The denomination is less effective evangelistically; the gain of members from other groups has slowed. "The controversy" causes people to either leave or shy away.

Student work will not escape the fallout. We can expect fewer paid personnel, shorter budgets, less building, fewer expensive programs, and more use of volunteers and bivocational persons. Thus, the vocation of campus minister is in peril.

As much as the use of volunteers in all areas of Southern Baptist life has been meaningful, it is at the point of campus ministry that volunteers are the most questionable. That question arises where continuity is imperative. Volunteers with little training and less experience have a tendency to build BSU programs around themselves. When they leave short-term service, their programs have a tendency to disappear, but volunteers are transient people who hope they create future permanent positions. Student ministry has become a popular vocation considered by seminary graduates, so leaders should look in these places for personnel. Because of the numbers Southern Baptist seminaries are now graduating as church positions decline, seminaries are fruitful vineyards to find trained personnel for new work.

Volunteers, particularly in the student arena, should be placed on campuses in newer territory areas with those states' personnel understanding that the purpose is to develop these campus programs until permanent help can be secured and financed.

Good examples of such volunteers are Rob Lee, now state BSU director of the Utah-Idaho Baptist Convention who began as a US-2 worker at Utah State in Logan, and Betsy Draper, a career home missionary at Massachusetts Institute of Technology who began her work as a Mission Corps volunteer in Boston.

There is a conviction among some that though the success of short-term volunteers has been an asset to campus ministry, there must be a continuation to develop those who plan to do this work as a lifetime ministry. Our seminaries, and other institutions, should joyfully shoulder the task of teaching outstanding young people that on the battleground of ideas comes the great challenge to show the Christian faith can shine in academia.

Meanwhile, Southern Baptists should not forget those campus ministers who have given their lives in the states commonly known as old territory areas—the deep South and Southwest. These groups have been the ones who have provided the personnel and finances for summer missions, special work groups, and evangelistic endeavors for those in newer territory areas. It would be wise to make them feel they are still important to the total ministry of Southern Baptists across the nation and around the world.

Little help is being given to them by National Department of Student Ministries because the people involved chose to concentrate on newer territory areas. There *should* be experts at NSM to work in developing areas of SBC. However, there *also should* be leaders there who can prophesy the trends of the future that baffle those who battle the minds in the great institutions where BSU started. Now is the time, with a new head of student ministries, to pursue a liaison in the form of a person who can relate to those thoughts and ideas that permeate older institutions of higher learning. There must continue to be a good word for the permanent campus minister in the old South.

Charles Johnson retired in 1994, and Bill Henry, an associate in the Baptist Sunday School Board Student Department, assumed the head of Baptist student ministries program. In a recent press release he urged Baptists to look anew at their investment in college students. Henry remarked when returning from a marketing conference in New York City:

> Corporations are realizing if they can invest in students and secure their brand loyalty, they have an excellent chance of keeping them as adults. If we can help Southern Baptists catch a vision for reaching college students, our denomination will reap the rewards for years to come. If we don't, we will lose our impact in the next generation.

> We think ministry to college students is not a luxury but the lifeblood of the next generation of churchmanship. How many thousands of students do Southern Baptists lose because they do not see the value of college students?

> Too many people have the attitude that college students will be trying so many things that it is a waste of money on them. But this is the last time these potential leaders will be together. Marketing people know they have a captive audience here. Sometimes I don't think Southern Baptists understand or appreciate the mission field of college students. They are more reachable now than they ever will be. They're idealistic—they want something to be called to that is significant, that is important. . . .

> I was won to the Lord as a freshman in college. I know first-hand the importance of college ministry. The ministry we are in is a holy ministry.[4]

Henry seemed to be reiterating what seventy-five years of BSU history has taught us. He emphasized four ideas that have flowed throughout this volume. First, Henry borrowed from Hazelwood's example of bicarbonate of soda. If BSU is going to continue its success, the product is going to have to be packaged for the student of the 1990s and for those generations that will follow in the twenty-first century. Second, he validated history by suggesting that students have never been a priority with the denomination. Third, our new leader was warning anew that the potential loss of a student generation means a loss in the next generation of leaders. Every phase of Baptist life—missionaries overseas and at home, agency leaders who have the task to visualize strategies for pastor and people in local congregations—will feel the loss. Last, Henry gave the strongest testimony of all. Being an idealistic and reachable freshman, he was "won to Christ." Someone on a college campus cared enough to introduce him to the God of Jesus Christ. Now, hopefully, he will lead the national student program into an excitable new millennium.

CONCLUSION

My silent thoughts and prayers are and will continue to be with present-day campus ministers in far-flung places and difficult circumstances. In my prayers, I have been reminded of a letter in James Michener's book, *Texas*. A bishop was writing to a local priest concerning stopping Christian work in that state: "I do not speak disparagingly of the friars who attempt to do God's work in these remote and depressing areas . . . but the numbers of Indians converting are minimal and to continue this fruitless effort will be financially and religiously unjustified. Close the mission."[5] Michener then became theological:

> What the priest overlooked in his accurate but harsh summary of those brave friars was the sincere interest Spain had shown in the souls of the Indians. But the greatest injustice in the bishop's judgment on the mission was that he did not take into account the nature of God or the workings of His will. God had not come to Texas in white robes attended by choirs of angels; He came as a toilworn Franciscan friar; He came as a mestizo woman lugging two bawling babies who would grow into stalwart men; he came sweating Himself over the vast amount of work to be done before the place could be civilized. All these were closer to Heaven than the bishop who wrote the letter would ever be.[6]

God did not arrive on college and university campuses when campus ministers—or US-2ers or semester and summer missionaries or Mission Service Corps volunteers—arrived. God was already there in a fear-enshrouded freshman, a cynical sophomore, a pseudo-intellectual junior, a sophisticated senior, and a secularized faculty.

Perhaps the rumor of God has dimmed to a flicker on the university campus, but the wind blows where it wills! The task is to arrive, strive, and cause the wind to flame that rumor into a blaze as we race into the unknown of the twenty-first century.

HAPPY ANNIVERSARY BSU!! You are worthy of a diamond in your seventy-fifth year.

APPENDIX A

The Philosophy and Objectives of Southern Baptist Student Work
December 1962

The Philosophy

The Christian witness of Southern Baptist student work in all institutions of higher learning is in response to our Lord's command to make known the gospel to all men.

This witness is an integral part of the nature and mission of the church. The role of the churches is indispensable to the maturing spiritual, moral, and intellectual lives of students and faculty members.

Because the university* is engaged in the search for truth, of which God is the source, the Christian perspective is essential to the realization of the ultimate purpose of higher education.

The unique nature of the university situation demands a specialized ministry by our denomination to the individuals in the campus community with their need for redemption and Christian nurture.

—J. P. Edmunds, "The Philosophy of Southern Baptist Student Work," *Quarterly Review,* 23 (January, February, and March 1963): 7.

*Used here to refer to all types of schools beyond the level of secondary education (except theological seminaries), such as: colleges, universities, service academies, professional schools, etc. [This statement was an asterisk insertion into the report.]

The Objectives

The basic objective is to motivate students and faculty members to commitment to Jesus Christ as Savior and Lord through:

1. Involving them in responsible church membership and in denominational understanding and participation.

2. Guiding them in worship and devotional experiences.

3. Involving them in the study of the biblical faith and Christian life.

4. Involving them in experiences of Christian community.

5. Guiding them in Christian witnessing.

6. Leading them to participate in Christian world missions.

7. Leading them to accept and practice the principles of Christian stewardship.

8. Leading them to examine academic disciplines from a Christian perspective.

9. Enlisting and training them for a life of Christian service.

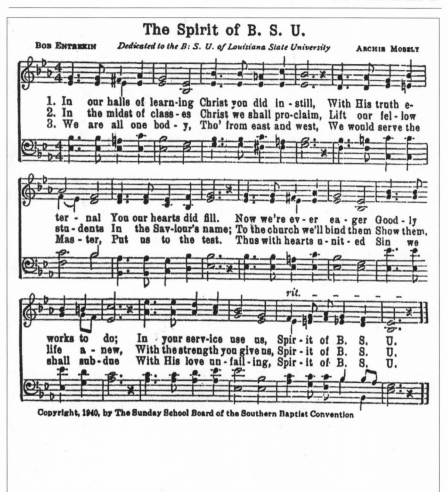

The Spirit of B. S. U.

BOB ENTREKIN   *Dedicated to the B: S. U. of Louisiana State University*   ARCHIE MOSELY

1. In our halls of learn-ing Christ you did in-still, With His truth e-
ter-nal You our hearts did fill. Now we're ev-er ea-ger Good-ly
works to do; In your serv-ice use us, Spir-it of B. S. U.

2. In the midst of class-es Christ we shall pro-claim, Lift our fel-low
stu-dents In the Sav-iour's name; To the church we'll bind them Show them,
life a-new, With the strength you give us, Spir-it of B. S. U.

3. We are all one bod-y, Tho' from east and west, We would serve the
Mas-ter, Put us to the test. Thus with hearts u-nit-ed Sin we
shall sub-due With His love un-fail-ing, Spir-it of B. S. U.

Copyright, 1940, by The Sunday School Board of the Southern Baptist Convention

Issued by the
DEPARTMENT OF STUDENT WORK
SUNDAY SCHOOL BOARD
— of the —
SOUTHERN BAPTIST CONVENTION
Nashville, Tennessee

ENDNOTES

Introduction

1. Claude Broach, *Dr. Frank* (Nashville: Broadman Press, 1950), 72.

2. Elton Trueblood, *The Company of the Committed* (New York: Harper and Row, 1961), 12.

3. Samuel Sanford Jr., *Ann Lee: Echoes of a Pilgrimage* (New Orleans: Dinstuhl Publishing Co., 1978), 2.

4. G. Avery Lee, "How the Churches Benefit from the Baptist Student Union" (address to the New Orleans Baptist Brotherhood, August 1964).

5. Kenneth Scott Latourette, *These Sought a Country* (New York: Harper and Row, 1950), 46.

6. Stewart Newman, *W. T. Conner, Theologian of the Southwest* (Nashville: Broadman Press, 1964), 80.

7. Ralph C. Dunlop, "The Ministry of a Local Church to the University," in *On the Work of the Ministry in University Communities*, edited by Richard N. Bender (Nashville: Board of Education, the Methodist Church, 1962), 89.

8. For further reading: Allan Bloom, *The Closing of the American Mind* (New York: Simon and Schuster, 1987). Christopher Lasch, *The Culture of Narcissism* (New York: W. W. Norton and Company, 1979). Arthur Levine, *When Dreams and Heroes Died* (San Francisco: Jossey-Bass Publishers, 1983).

9. For further reading: Nancy Tatom Ammermam, *Baptist Battles: Social Change and Religious Conflict in the Southern Baptist Convention* (New Brunswick, N.J.: Rutgers University Press, 1990). Grady Couthen, *What Happened to the Southern Baptist Convention?* (Macon, Ga.: Smyth and Helwys, 1993). Walter B. Shurden, editor, *The Struggle for the Soul of the SBC* (Macon, Ga.: Smyth and Helwys, 1990).

10. John Cantelon, *A Protestant Approach to the Campus Ministry* (Philadelphia: Westminster Press, 1964), 84.

11. Donald G. Shockley, *Campus Ministry—The Church Beyond Itself* (Louisville, Ky.: The Westminster/John Knox Press, 1989), 125.

Chapter One

1. Kenneth Scott Latourette, *These Sought a Country* (New York: Harper and Row, 1950), 46.

2. Clarence Shedd, *Two Centuries of Student Christian Movements* (New York: Association Press, 1934), 1.

3. Clyde L. Manschreck, *A History of Christianity in the World* (Englewood Cliffs, N.J.: Prentice-Hall, Inc., 1974), 337.

4. Donald G. Shockley, *Campus Ministry—The Church Beyond Itself* (Louisville, Ky.: the Westminster/John Knox Press, 1989), 26.

5. Clarence Shedd, *The Church Follows Its Students* (New Haven, Conn.: Yale University Press, 1938), 1–2.

6. Charles Barnes, "The Administration of the Baptist Student Center on the State or Private College Campus" (doctoral dissertation, Southwestern Baptist Theological Seminary, Fort Worth, 1958), 13.

7. Shedd, *Two Centuries,* 3–13.

8. Seymour A. Smith, *The American College Chaplaincy* (New York: Association Press, 1954), 1.

9. Shedd, *Two Centuries,* 48.

10. *The Daily Beacon* of the University of Tennessee, "Baptist Students Find Fellowship, Friends at Union" 1994 Vol. 67, No. 67, 1.

11. Jane Young Poster, *Reckless for Christ* (Greenville, S.C.: A Press, 1994), 12–13.

12. David M. Howard, *Student Power in World Missions* (Downer's Grove, Ill.: InterVarsity, 1979), 73–75.

13. Watson A. Omulogol, *The Student Volunteer Movement: Its History and Contributions* (Wheaton, Ill.: Wheaton College, 1967), 18.

14. Shedd, *Two Centuries,* 92.

15. Howard C. Hopkins, *History of the Y.M.C.A. in North America* (New York: Association Press, 1951), 38.

16. Shedd, *Two Centuries,* 145–46.

17. Sabin Landry, "Southern Baptists Meeting Life Needs of Students in Tax-Supported Colleges" (doctoral dissertation, the Southern Baptist Theological Seminary), 1954, 36.

18. Shedd, *Two Centuries,* 382–422.

19. Joseph W. Cochran, "State Universities and Religious Denominations," *Religious Education*, 4 (November and December 1910): 169–70.

20. Claude Broach, *Dr. Frank* (Nashville: Broadman Press, 1950), 98.

21. Joseph W. Cochran, "Preparation for Leadership—Conditions and Plans for the Religious Welfare of Students in Universities," *Religious Education*, 5 (January and February 1911): 120–21.

Chapter Two

1. Clarence Shedd, *The Church Follows Its Students* (New Haven: Yale University Press, 1983), 12–13.

2. *Southern Baptist Convention Annual 1918*, 424.

3. Andrew Q. Allen, "A Brief History of the Baptist Student Missionary Movement and the Baptist Student Union in Texas" (master's thesis, Southwestern Baptist Theological Seminary, Fort Worth, 1929), 14.

4. G. Avery Lee, *"Where Christian Ideas Take Shape in People"* (New Orleans: Seventy-fifth Anniversary History of St. Charles Avenue Baptist Church, 1898–1973), 43–44.

5. *Texas Baptist Convention Annual 1919,* 16.

6. *Mississippi Baptist Convention Annual 1919,* 92.

7. Claude Broach, *Dr. Frank* (Nashville: Broadman Press, 1950), 72.

8. Frank H. Leavell, "An Evaluation of the Baptist Student Union" (Nashville: Leavell Papers, D–C Library, Sunday School Board, May 1927), 2–3.

9. "Leavell Papers," Box 2.

10. Broach, *Dr. Frank,* 91.

11. Proceedings of All-Southern Baptist Student Conference, *Christ, Master of My Generation* (Nashville: Sunday School Board, 1927), 8.

12. H. D. Bollinger, interview with the author, May 3, 1965.

13. T. G. Dunning, "An International Citizen," *Baptist Student,* 29 (June 1950): 8–9.

14. "Leavell Papers," Box 3.

15. Broach, *Dr. Frank,* 92–93.

16. Robert Denny, Chester Durham, G. Avery Lee, and Howard Rees, correspondence to the author, July 19, September 17, July 18, July 25, 1965, respectively.

17. G. Avery Lee, correspondence to the author, April 17, 1965.

18. Johnni Johnson, "Maximum Christianity," *Baptist Student,* 29 (June 1950): 25, citing Leavell's editorial, February 1940 from same publication.

19. Claude Broach, correspondence to the author, August 16, 1965.

Chapter Three

1. Frank H. Leavell, "Serving the Religious Needs of Students in American Colleges," (Nashville: Leavell Papers, D–C Library, Sunday School Board, January 1935), 9.

2. Frank H. Leavell, "The Philosophy and Program of Southern Baptist Student Work" (Nashville: Sunday School Board, May 1947), 11.

3. Ibid., 12.

4. Leavell, "Serving," 10.

5. Leavell, "The Student Viewpoint," *Baptist Student,* 1 (September and October 1922): 1–2.

6. Leavell, "The Philosophy," 10.

7. Claude Broach, *Dr. Frank* (Nashville: Broadman Press, 1950), 90–91.

8. Ibid., 98.

9. Frank H. Leavell, *Baptist Student Union Methods* (Nashville: Sunday School Board, 1927), 81–84.

10. Doyle J. Baird, "The Place of the Baptist Student Union Director on a Tax-Supported College or University Campus" (doctoral dissertation, Southwestern Baptist Theological Seminary, Fort Worth, 1961), 185.

11. Tom Logue, personal correspondence to the author, July 23, 1965.

12. Howard Rees, personal correspondence to the author, June 11, 1965.

13. Ibid.

14. Frank H. Leavell, "A Resume of Five Years" (Nashville: Leavell Papers, D–C Library, Sunday School Board, May 1927), 1.

15. W. F. Howard, "After Fifty Years," *Student* (January 1972): 20–21.

16. Ibid., 21, 29.

Chapter Four

1. Richard H. Ostheimer, *A Statistical Analysis of the Organization of Higher Education* (New York: Columbia Press, 1951), 3.

2. George L. Earnshaw, editor, *The Campus Ministry* (Valley Forge, Penn.: Judson Press, 1964), 295.

3. George Jones, "Report of the Commission on Commuters" (Nashville: Sunday School Board, 1959), 1.

4. Nell Magee, "The Associational Student Work Committee," *Quarterly Review* (January, February, and March 1963): 35.

5. John J. O'Connell, "The Case for the Asphalt Campus," *This Week* (June 5, 1966): 2.

6. Richard N. Bender, editor, *On the Work of the Ministry in University Communities* (Nashville: Division of Higher Education, the Methodist Church, 1962), 91.

7. Ibid., 93

8. I was chair of this group, but as I will write, a *correct* objection of the state student directors about having no representatives on the original commissions caused a reorganization of this work. Dr. Keegan assumed that local campus directors were more knowledgeable about new fragmentation in the campus community. The state directors did not agree. Keegan was embarrassed by all this, but had the courage to admit his mistake and undertook other ways to complete the task. The Expansion Commission was deleted as such and assumed a new entity composed of a mixture of local and state directors. The state directors finally in 1962 voted and passed the unified philosophical statement.

9. Howard Bramlette, "Graduate Student Recruitment," *Key News*, 11 (Summer 1966): 17.

10. James O. Cansler, "Report of the Commission on Graduate Students" (Nashville: Student Department, Sunday School Board, 1959), 1.

11. Bender, *On the Work*, 207.

12. Kate Havener Mueller, *Student Personnel Work in Higher Education* (Boston: Houghton Mifflin Company, 1961), 487.

13. Reginald W. Wheeler, editor, *The Foreign Student in America* (New York: Association Press, 1925), 192.

14. Howard Bramlette, "The Care and Nurture of Southern Baptist Faculty Members," *Baptist Program* (June 1996): 19.

15. George L. Earnshaw, editor, *The Campus Ministry* (Valley Forge, Penn.: Judson Press, 1964), 140.

16. Bramlette, "The Care and Nurture."

17. Cansler, "Report of the Commission," 2.

Chapter Five

1. Udell Smith, *The State Student Directors Association* (from his files and subsequent correspondence, May 1996). Smith served twice as president of this group.

2. Ibid.

3. Ibid.

4. Marianna C. Brown, *Sunday School Movements in America*, second edition (New York: Fleming H. Revell Company 1901), 45.

5. Jane Poster Young, *Reckless for Christ* (Greenville, S.C.: A Press, 1994), 30, 31.

6. H. Eugene Maston, "A Report in the Interest of Baptist Student Work in the Northeastern Baptist Association" (New York: Columbia University, 1961), 2.

7. Ibid. 3.

8. William Junker, "Pioneer Student Work to Benefit from Sunday School Board Action," *Key News,* 7 (May 1962): 1–3.

9. Corbin Gwaltney, "To Keep Pace With America," *Editorial Projects for Education,* 1 (January 1966): 1–16.

10. S. L. Harris, "Report of the Commission on Married Students" (Nashville: Student Department, Sunday School Board, 1959), 1.

11. George L. Earnshaw, editor, *The Campus Ministry* (Valley Forge, Penn.: Judson Press, 1964), 281.

12. Ibid.

13. *Southern Baptist Convention Annual 1960*, 186.

14. Samuel Sanford, "Report of the Expansion Commission" (Nashville: Student Department, Sunday School Board, 1959), 1–2.

15. Ibid., 1.

16. J. P. Edmunds, "The Work of 'Study Group 1,'" *Quarterly Review*, 23 (January, February, and March 1963): 8.

17. Ibid.

Chapter Six

1. Willliam Junker, "Milestones in Student Ministries," *Quarterly Review,* 32 (April–June 1972): 9.

2. Samuel Sanford, "Report of the Expansion Commission" (Nashville: Student Department, Sunday School Board, 1959), 4.

3. Robert A. Sanks, "Ministry to Married Students" in *On the Work of the Ministry in Academic Communities,* edited by Richard Bender (Nashville: Division of Higher Education, the Methodist Church, 1962), 95.

4. Walter Shurden, personal correspondence to the author, August 29, 1995.

5. J. P. Edmunds, "The Philosophy of Southern Baptist Student Work," *Quarterly Review,* 23 (January–March 1963): 7.

6. Deane William Ferm, "Negative Images of the Church in the Academic Community," in *On the Work of the Ministry in Academic Communities,* edited by Richard Bender (Nashville: Division of Higher Education, the Methodist Church, 1962), 217.

7. Doyle Baird, editor, *Resource Book for Workers with Students in Churches Affiliated with the Southern Baptist Convention* (Nashville: Student Department, Sunday School Board, 1964), 32.

8. Udell Smith, "The Growing Responsibility of the State Student Directors' Association" (Alexandria: Student Division, Louisiana Baptist Convention, February 1962), 6–7.

9. Don Hammonds, chairperson, *Report of the Student Work Task Force* (Atlanta: Baptist Home Mission Board, May 1990), 16.

10. Rabun L. Brantley, editor, "Student Ministry Study Requested" (Nashville: *The Southern Baptist Educator,* 28 (July and August 1964): 8.

11. *Southern Baptist Convention Annual* 1961, 57–8.

12. The Education Commission, "Southern Baptist Campus Directory," *Southern Baptist Educator,* 24 (May and June 1960): 5–6.

13. Penrose St. Amant, "Preface to a Philosophy of Southern Baptist Higher Education—Faith and Learning," *Southern Baptist Educator,* 30 (May and June 1966): 3.

Chapter Seven

1. For further illumination on the 1920s, see Paul Johnson, *Modern Times* (New York: HarperCollins, 1992), 203–29.

2. In 1962 I left Louisiana Tech to be the coordinator of Baptist student work for the schools in New Orleans and to teach campus ministry at New Orleans Baptist Theological Seminary. One of the activities prior to leaving Ruston was a unified service of all the Baptist churches with me preaching. That evening I titled my remarks "The Honeymoon is Over." The letters received from these wonderful folk were interesting over the next two or three years. The gist of most was "I didn't believe a thing you said that evening, but I do now!"

3. Fred Witty was the BSU director at the University of Louisville when a young African-American student named Emmanuel McCall came to the BSU center. This was the beginning of the integration era. Witty was relieved of his duties because of McCall's participation. He later went to East Tennessee State University and retired from there after an illustrious career. McCall became one, if not *the*, most important person in leading the SBC to cooperate with National

Baptists—three African-American denominations—and other such groups through Atlanta's Baptist HMB. He has never forgotten Witty's action nor has his love for BSU diminished. McCall is now senior pastor of Friendship Baptist Church in Atlanta and is a past National president of the Southern Baptist Theological Seminary's Alumni Association.

4. "The Jesus Revolution," *Time*, 97 (June 21, 1971): 59.

5. Reference to *Whole Earth Catalog*

6. Walker L. Knight, compiler, *Jesus People Come Alive* (Wheaton, Ill.: Tyndale House Publishers, 1971), 112.

7. *Time*, 61.

8. Arthur Blessitt came through Monroe, Louisiana, in 1970 with his entourage of "Crossing America." (He carried a wooden cross on this trek.) Somehow, the BSU at Northeast Louisiana University became involved. Some students left school to join his group; others began to speak in tongues; still others learned to "love Jesus" but their ethical and moral lives left much to be desired.

A previously large, thriving BSU was torn asunder by the appearance of Blessitt. By 1971 this religious group was almost nonexistent. Those who remained were so psychologically scarred and fear-frozen (their energy sapped) they could not find the strength to provide leadership for program rejuvenation. This is one example of the detriment the Jesus people perpetrated on Southern Baptists' student programs.

9. Knight, *Jesus People Come Alive,* 121–22.

10. *The Tower* (St. Charles Avenue Baptist Church bulletin, New Orleans, Louisiana, April 30, 1967), 1.

11. The previous two sections are condensed versions of articles I wrote for the Conventionwide Student Department in 1968–69. One was a *Key News* article titled "The 'New' Student in Transition"; the other was a pamphlet called "The Times They Are A' Changin.'"

Chapter Eight

1. William Junker, "Milestones in Student Ministries," *Quarterly Review,* 32 (April–June, 1972): 10.

2. Charles Roselle, "Here We Are in Student Ministries—," *Quarterly Review,* 32 (April, May, June 1972): 7.

3. Jack U. Harwell, "Florida Student Minister Has Winning Programs at Church, School," *Baptist Today* (March 9, 1995): 19.

4. Charles W. Deweese, editor, *Defining Baptist Convictions—Guidelines for the Twenty-First Century* (Franklin, Tenn.: Providence House Publishers, 1996), 38.

Chapter Nine

1. Ellen Goodman, "New Year Arrives Wary, Worried," *Monroe* (La.) *News-Star World,* January 1, 1981.

2. David Nyhan, "Why Young People Like Ronald Reagan," *Arkansas Gazette*, October 1, 1984.

3. John Naisbitt, *Megatrends* (New York: Warner Books, 1984), 279.

4. The writer spent the last five years of his ministry (1980–1985) during his allotted time away from the campus speaking to groups of states' campus ministers, teaching J Terms at seminaries, and writing research papers for agencies on the subject of the chapter. In 1981 he first spoke about the coming affects of "the controversy" on campus ministry. The basic thesis was "This won't go away as other SBC controversies had in the past." Only a few believed! He returned to some states and always began, "As I said several years ago . . ." The reply generally was "We heard you; we didn't want to believe it."

5. Robert M. Baird, "The Creative Role of Doubt in Religion," *Journal of Religion and Health*, 19 (Fall 1980): 172–79.

6. Ronald Brown, "Religious Hungers of the Young Adult," (mimeograph for Church-Campus Seminars, 1983): 2.

7. From notes of Ferris Jordan's lecture to a campus ministry class during a J Term at New Orleans seminary in 1985 that he and the writer mentioned above co-taught.

8. Ronald Brown, "Religious Hungers," 2.

9. "A PT Conversation with James Fowler," *Psychology Today* (November 1983): 56.

10. Ibid., p. 56.

11. Ircel Harrison, "A Book Review: James Fowler's *Stages of Faith*," *Campus Minister* (Spring 1983): 66–68.

12. *Southern Baptist Annual* 1982, 357.

13. Samuel Sanford, "Forty Years Between Town and Gown—A Theological Perspective," *Campus Minister* (Winter 1978): 27–28.

14. Leo Armstrong, "The Place of Church and BSU," (Church-Campus Seminar at Northeast Louisiana University, Monroe, August 23, 1981).

15. Robert Magee, interview by author for a research paper, March 1985.

16. L. D. Kenney, "The Real Task of Christian Education," *Baptist Program* (February 1985): 19.

17. Randall Balmer, "Churchgoing: Collegiate United Methodist Church in Ames, Iowa," *Christian Century* (May 11, 1994): 492.

Chapter Ten

1. The Carnegie Foundation, *Campus Life: In Search of Community*, (Lawrenceville, N.J.: Princeton University Press, 1990), 1.

2. Ibid., 1, 63–67.

3. Donald G. Shockley, *Campus Ministry: The Church Beyond Itself* (Louisville: Westminister/ John Knox Press, 1989), 53. Used by permission.

4. William H. Willimon, "Reaching and teaching the abandoned generation," *Christian Century* (October 20, 1993): 1016–19.

5. "Duke: To Be or Not to Be a Party School," *Atlanta Constitution,* October 23, 1993.

6. Willimon, "Reaching," 1018.

7. Jack Greever, "Meeting the Needs of Today's Students" in *Here's Help for You,* edited by Presnell H. Wood, 120.

8. Jack U. Harwell, editor, "Daniel Vestal's Legacy at Tallowood Foreshadows his CBF Future," *Baptist Today* (March 20, 1997): 3.

Chapter Eleven

1. Frederick Buechner, *The Sacred Journey* (San Francisco: Harper and Row, 1982), 111.

2. William J. Bennett, editor and commentator, *The Book of Virtues* (New York: Simon and Schuster, 1993), 269.

3. For an excellent primer on creativity, see David Campbell, *Take the Road to Creativity and Get Off your Rear End* (Niles, Ill.: Argus Communications, 1987).

4. Bennett, *The Book,* 347–48.

5. "Minorities in Higher Education" in *American Council of Education* (Sixth Annual Status Report, Washington, D.C., 1987), 3.

6. Scott Hudgins, "The Changing Religious Commitment of African-American Students," (paper read at Ridgecrest Baptist Assembly, Ridgecrest, N.C., August 1991).

7. Donald D. Shockley, *Campus Ministry: The Church Beyond Itself . . .* , 123.

Epilogue

1. "Student Ministry," *Baptist Message,* 111 (October 31, 1996): 2.

2. Nicholas Evans, *The Horse Whisperer* (New York: Bantam Doubleday Dell Publishing Group, Inc., 1995), 123.

3. Charles Walker, editor, *Campus Minister,* 17 (Winter 1995): 6.

4. "Southern Baptists Must 'Invest' in College Students, Leader Insists," *Baptist Message,* 5.

5. James A. Michener, *Texas* (New York: Random House, Inc., 1985), 180. Used by permission.

6. Ibid., 180–81.

ABOUT THE AUTHOR

Samuel Sanford Jr. is a retired Baptist campus minister, having spent his whole career—thirty-nine years—on four campuses and in two medical schools in Louisiana. They were Southeastern Louisiana University in Hammond (1946–1950), in which Sanford was their first full-time campus minister; Louisiana Polytechnic Institute in Ruston (1950–1962); Tulane-Newcomb-Loyola Universities and the Medical Center of New Orleans (1962–1971), which included Louisiana State University and Tulane medical schools; and Northeast Louisiana University in Monroe (1971–1985). The past decade he has served as a contract worker for the Special Ministries Department of the Home Mission Board, with particular duties involving campus "US-2ers."

Sanford was educated at Louisiana State University (B.S., 1943), Southwestern and New Orleans Baptist theological seminaries (M.R.E., 1946 and Ed.D., 1967) with sabbaticals at Southern Seminary and in Mansfield College at Oxford University, England.

He was Special Instructor in Campus Ministries at New Orleans Baptist Theological Seminary from 1962 to 1971. During that same period he taught theology at Tulane University and lectured and wrote on medical ethics for the medical centers in New Orleans. He coauthored *The World of Medicine—An Invitation to Dialogue* in 1970.

On the denominational level, Sanford has written extensively for the *Student*. He was a book reviewer for the *Key News* several years. Other campus-ministry publications have included his material, along with articles for other departments of the Sunday School Board. His book titled *Ann Lee: Echoes of a Pilgrimage* was completed in 1978. *Only the Rocks Live Forever*, a memoir, is in progress.

Sanford served on two Conventionwide Baptist Student Union study groups—1959 and 1969—which were for philosophical assurances of the able concepts of Southern Baptists' campus-ministry program.

He was among the first campus ministers to serve as moderator of a Baptist association. He holds membership in Who's Who in the South.

Civic duties performed have been cochairman of Louisiana's Heart Association, president of his children's Parent-Teacher's Association, and a three-year term on Louisiana's Governor's Developmental Disabilities Council.

159

Local church responsibilities have included deacon service, adult Sunday School teacher, and member of finance and budget committees. Also, he served twice on Long-Range Church Planning committees.

In 1997 he will have been married to Esther (Oden) Sanford for fifty years. They have three children: Robert Maston of Houston, Esther Ann (deceased 1990), and David Raymond of New Orleans. The Sanfords have six grandchildren.